STUDY NOTES

UGC

PSYCHOLOGY
(PAPER - II)

VOLUME - 4

Content Table

Unit No	Unit	Page No
10.	Emerging Areas	2–100

UNIT – 10

EMERGING AREAS

EMERGING AREAS

What is Issues of Gender, Poverty, Disability, and Migration: Cultural bias and discrimination. Stigma, Marginalization, and Social Suffering; Child Abuse and Domestic violence?
Issues of Gender, Poverty, Disability, and Migration: Cultural bias and discrimination. Stigma, Marginalization, and Social Suffering; Child Abuse and Domestic violence

Issues of Gender

ANNCREASE GENDER REPRESENTATION/ GENDER BALANCE
One of the main objectives set by UNI Global Union, through its Equal Opportunities Department has been to attain productive development based on gender equality. We regard this principle as essential to achieving sustainable development and true social justice for everyone.

The Equal Opportunites Department carries out programmes, campaigns and other activities in order to fulfil this goal, both within the organization and among our affiliates.

VIOLENCE AGAINST WOMEN
The socially and culturally built hierarchy between the genders holds certain power relationships. Any power relationship is asymmetrical by definition, i.e. one of the subjects of the relationship has power and the other one does not.

Usually, men are socially regarded as being of higher value. This asymmetrical situation is present in many areas of social life andcan lead to violence (physical, verbal, or psychological). Studies show that more than 1/3 of the women around the world have experienced violence at some point in their lives and it can happen at the workplace.

SEXUAL HARASSMENT
Sexual harassment is a form of violence that through a show of power intimidates, humiliates, and affects another person's dignity. This behavior is sexual in nature (physical contacts, sexual advances, comments and jokes with sexual content, exhibiting pornographic material or making inappropriate comments) and undesired; it is perceived by the victim as a condition to keep thejob, or as one that creates a hostile, intimidating, and humiliating work environment.

THE WAGE GAP
One of the areas at the workplace where gender differences are seen is the difference in the remuneration that men and women workers receive for work of equal value. A study by the InternationalLabour Organization in 2013 shows that the global wage gap is 23%.

However, this number does not account for the millions of women working in the informal economy with no protection. Also, many countries lack reliable statistics to prepare more accurate reports, therefore, this already high figure will be even higher.Access to education continues to be key to bridging the wage gap. However, it is not the only instrument, since women with higher education are at the ends of the gap with their male peer. For that reason, UNI has pledged to work to make ILO Convention 100 requiring equal remuneration for men and women workers for work of equal value effective in every work site.

WOMEN'S HEALTH
Health is a universal human right. That's why, irrespective of religion, age or where we live, we have a right to the information and the healthcare services that allow us to care for our bodies and our quality of life.

It is not just being free of illnesses, but also having access toreasonable standards of living, housing, food, decent work, as well as appropriate level of medical assistance so that we can develop our full potential as individuals.

To be able to truly achieve gender equality, we need to look at the health and well-being of women. This is a precondition for thepromotion of the sustainable growth of our communities.

WORK - LIFE BALANCE
Globalization of the economy has brought about changes in the labour market structure and labour organization, which had remained stable throughout the 20th century. The traditional model of sexual division of labour had placed productive tasks (supporting and providing for the family) in the hands of men and reproductive ones in the hands of women (caring for children and the elderly, housekeeping chores.)

Today, women increasingly share the provider role with men. However, there has not been a similar change in the distribution of domestic work. For that reason, women with both roles (productive and reproductive) work more hours than men, get less rest, and ar burdened with a heavy workload that puts their health at risk and limits their chances of developing a professional career.

We must then reflect upon these issues and devise   policies intended to balance work and family life to overcome gender inequalities, so that both men and women may have access to a fullfamily life and a professional career.

In many parts of the world, technological innovations such as artificial intelligence (AI), robotics and machine learning are impacting society. These new technologies allow us   to communicate faster, share information and feel closer to each other. They are, today, an essential part of our lives and provide us with unprecedented opportunities to advance in areas ranging from education to political participation.

Its use and dissemination is so common that we do not see the impact they have on women. Technology is a reflection of reality, and if we do not work to eradicate the inequalities and prejudices that they transmit, we will continue to widen those gaps we want to close today.

The UNI Equal Opportunities department has begun to address the issue of the impact of digitalization on women by writing conceptual documents that will help continue discussions on this issue.

Our first document: "Digitization from a gender perspective", was intended to explain what digitalization means, and how it will affect the world of work, in particular, working women.

A second document: "The road to digitalization without gender" was written as part of a collaboration with the European group of experts"Friends of Europe" for its report "Policy options for a digital era". This second document explores further the impact of technolog and artificial intelligence on women, the prejudices that permeate the development of these technologies and how they contribute to the gender gap, promoting possible solutions to these issues.

GENDER ISSUES IN INDIA:

Political Economy

In 2016, India ranked 130 out of 146 in the Gender Inequality Index released by the UNDP. It is evident that a stronger turn in political discourse is required, taking into consideration both public and private spaces. The normalization of intra-household violence is a huge detriment to the welfare of women. Crimes against women have doubled in the period between 1991 and 2011. NFHS data reports that 37 per cent of married women in India haveexperienced physical or sexual violence by a spouse while 40 per cent have experienced physical, sexual or emotional violence by a spouse. While current policy discourse recommends employment asa form of empowerment for women, data presents a disturbingcorrelation between female participation in labour force and their exposure to domestic violence. The NFHS-3 reports that women employed at any time in the past 12 months have a much higher prevalence of violence (39-40 per cent) than women who were not employed (29 per cent). The researchers advocate a multi-faceted approach to women's empowerment beyond mere labour force participation, taking into consideration extra-household bargaining power.

Gender inequality extends across various facets of society. Political participation is often perceived as a key factor to rectify this situation. However, gender bias extends to electoral politics and representative governance as well. The relative difference between male and female voters is the key to understanding gende inequality in politics. While the female voter turnout has been steadily increasing, the number of female candidates fielded byparties has not increased. More women contest as independents, which does not provide the cover for extraneous costs otherwise available when they are part of a political party.

However, women also act as agents of political change for other women. In the Bihar elections in 2005, when re-elections were held,the percentage of female voters had increased from 42.5 to 44.5 percent while those of male voters declined from 50 to 47 per cent in the interim period of eight months. As a direct result, 37 per cent of the constituencies saw anti-incumbency voting. The average growthrate of women voters was nearly three times in those constituencieswhere there was a difference in the winning party. District-wisedisaggregation of voter registration also supports this hypothesis in the case of Bihar indicating the percolation of the winds of change. This illustration proves that women are no longer under   the complete control of the men in their family in terms of electoral participation. The situation is only bound to improve from here. With the introduction of Electronic Voting Machines (EVMs), vulnerable sections like women now have more freedom of choice in their vote.Further, poll related incidents of violence against women have significantly decreased since the phased introduction of EVMs across multi-level elections in India.

Extending the conversation to political representation is the next phase in the conversation. Women make up merely 22 per cent of lower houses in parliaments around the world and in India, this number is less than half at 10.8 per cent in the outgoing Lok Sabha.A steady increase in female voter participation has been observed across India, wherein the sex ratio of voters (number of female voters vis-à-vis male) has increased from 715 in the 1960s to 883 I the 2000s. Our studies have shown that women are more likely to contest elections in states with a skewed gender ratio. In the case ofmore developed states, they seek representation through voting leading to an increase in voter participation.

The situation can be rectified by providing focused reservation for those constituencies with a skewed sex ratio. Reducing the entry costs (largely non-pecuniary in nature – cultural barriers, lack of exposure) for women in order to create a pipeline of female leaders is another solution. These missing women, either as voters or leaders point to the gross negligence of women at all ages.

FINANCIAL INCLUSION

In the developing world, women have traditionally been the focus of efforts of financial inclusion. They have proved to be better borrowers (40 per cent of Grameen Bank's clients were women in 1983. By 2000, the number had risen to 90 per cent) – largely attributed to the fact that they are less mobile as compared to men and more susceptible to peer pressure. However, institutions inmicrofinance are exposed to the trade-off between market growth and social development since having more female clients lead tothe inevitable drip-down of social incentives. As an attempt to overcome this hurdle, a larger role can be played by donors with a gender driven agenda, for the financial inclusion sector will drive theidea further.

Gendered contextualisation of products is highly necessary for microfinance institutions (MFIs) – men and women do not ascribe tochoices in a similar fashion. Trends emerging from prior research indicates that when health insurance coverage was held under the MFI sector, by both men and women, women benefited from the coverage only so far as they were the holders and not using spousa status (if their husbands were insured). Thus healthcare seeking behaviour becomes an important factor to be considered in insurance coverage under the MFIs.

The JAM trinity – Jan Dhan Yojana, Aadhar, Mobile – can be used to improve financial inclusion from a gender perspective as well.The metrics to consider would be the number of Jan Dhan accountsheld by women, percentage of women holding Aadhar cards and access to mobile connectivity for women.

HEALTH

In terms of healthcare focusing on women, the Janani Suraksha Yojana (JSY) and National Health Mission are vital to the policy landscape. The JSY has improved maternal healthcare in Indiathrough the emphasis on institutional deliveries. Increase of 22 per cent in deliveries in government hospitals, was mirrored by an 8 per cent decline in childbirth at private hospitals and a 16 per cent decline in childbirth at home. The National Health Mission's ASHA led to greater awareness and education of pregnant women as well as an increase in institutional maternal and neonatal healthcare. Improved infrastructure for maternal and neo-natal has been observed in community hospitals, in addition to the introduction of ambulance services.

A gendered increase in seek care is observed with a large 13 per cent increase in the number of women who report being sick in the last 15 days, driving the overall reportage. Further, an eight per centdecline in rural women seeking private healthcare, has been reported, while a 58 per cent increase in women seekinghospitalization has been reported. Further disaggregated, the data shows a 75.7 per cent increase for rural women seeking healthcare.The overall increase in usage of public hospitals is almost entirel driven by rural women who saw an increase of 24.6 per cent in utilisation of public hospitals over the 10 years (2004-2014). Our results show that the JSY had a significant, positive impact onoverall hospitalisation of women in India. It increased the probability of a woman being hospitalised by approximately 1.3 per cent.

The healthcare sector in India has largely focused on maternalhealthcare for women. The importance of research on mental healthhas been ignored in policy discourse. The significant relationship that mental health bears on violence has also been explored in further research. Every fifth suicide in India is that of a housewife (18 per cent overall) – the reportage of suicide deaths has been most consistent among housewives as a category, than other categories. India is the country with the largest rate of female deaths due to 'intentional violence'.

Our work on childhood violence shows that girls are twice more likely to face sexual violence than boys before the age of 18. Larger the population of educated females in the country, lesser is the incidence of childhood violence at home – including lesser violent discipline, physical punishment as well as psychological aggression.Additionally, the lifetime experience of sexual violence by girls is strongly correlated with the adolescent fertility rate in a country. Further, a strong relationship is observed between female experience of sexual violence and female labour force participation within a country. The results show that the higher the labour force participation by women in a country, the higher is the incidence of sexual violence against them.

This could be indicative of adverse working conditions within labour markets, and the difficulty   of access to labour markets by young women in a country

POVERTY IN INDIA

Two-thirds of people in India live in poverty: 68.8% of the Indian population lives on less than $2 a day. Over 30% even have less than $1.25 per day available - they are considered   extremely poor. This makes the Indian subcontinent one of the poorest countries in the world; women and children, the weakest membersof Indian society, suffer most.

India is the second most populous country after China with about billion people and isthe seventh largest country in the world withan area of 3,287,000 km². The highly contrasted country has enjoyed growth rates of up to 10% over many years and is one of the largest economies in the world, with a gross domestic product (GDP) of 1,644 billion US dollars. But only a small percentage of theIndian population has benefited from this impressive   economic boom so far, as the majority of people in India are still   living in abject poverty.

Poverty in India: from the village to the slum

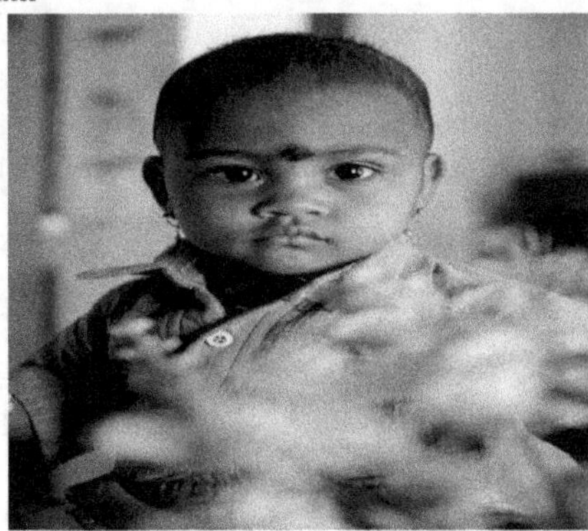

More than 800 million people in India are considered poor. Most of them live in the countryside and keep afloat with odd jobs. The lack of employment which provides alivable wage in rural areas is driving many Indians into rapidlygrowing metropolitan areas such as Bombay, Delhi, Bangalore o Calcutta. There, most of them expect a life of poverty and despair inthe mega-slums, made up of millions of corrugated ironworks, without sufficient drinking water supply, without garbage disposal and in many cases without electricity. The poor hygiene conditions are the cause of diseases such as cholera, typhus and dysentery, inwhich especially children suffer and die.

Poverty in India impacts children, families and individuals in   a variety of different ways through:
- High infant mortality
- Malnutrition
- Child labour
- Lack of education
- Child marriage
- HIV / AIDS

The high infant mortality

1.4 million children die each   year   in India before   their   fifth birthday. In addition to Nigeria, Pakistan, the Democratic

Republic of the Congo and China, India is one of the countries with the highest child mortality rates. Pneumonia, malaria and diarrheal diseases as well as chronic malnutrition are the most frequent causes of death.

Malnutrition - not even a bowl of rice a da India is one of the world's top countries when it comes to malnutrition: More than 200 million people don't have sufficient access to food, including 61 million children. 7.8 million infants werefound to have a birth weight of less than 2.5 kilograms - alarming figures for a country commonly referred to as the emerging market.

Child labour - no time to play and learn
Although child labour for children under the age of 14 in India is prohibited by law, according to official figures, 12.5 million children between the ages of 5 and 14 are working. Aid agencies assume that in reality, there are many more estimating that 65 million children between 6 and 14 years do not go to school. Instead, in order to secure survival, it is believed that Indian children contribute to the livelihood of their families; they work in the field, in factories,in quarries, in private households and in prostitution

Lack of education - no opportunities without education
According to UNICEF, about 25% of children in India have no access to education. The number of children excluded from schoolis higher among girls than boys. Although women and men aretreated equally under Indian law, girls and women, especially in the lower social caste, are considered inferior and are oppressed by their fathers, brothers and husbands. Without education, the chanceof finding a living wage from employment in India is virtually hopeless.

Child marriage - the early end of childhood
In spite of banning minors from marrying in 2006, it is still widespread in many regions of India. The main leaders in this practice are young girls, who are still children themselves and become mothers too early. Many of them die at birth. According to an investigation by the medical journal The Lancet, 44.5% of girls are still married in India before they are of legal age. Due to poverty, many parents encourage early marriages for their daughters in hopes of better lives for them.

DISABILITY IN INDIA

As per Census 2011, in India, out of the 121 Cr population, about 2.68 Cr persons are 'disabled' which is 2.21% of the total population. In an era where 'inclusive development' is being emphasised as the right path towards sustainable development,focussed initiatives for the welfare of disabled persons are essential.This emphasises the need for strengthening disability statistics in the Country.

There are ample reasons for developing a sound national disability statistics. Information on their socio - demographic profile is essential for welfare of disabled persons. Information about their functional status is important to identify needs since two individuals with the same impairment may face different types of difficulties in undertaking certain activities, and so have different needs that require different kinds of interventions.

Functional status data is essential for determining the broader socialneeds of persons with disabilities, such as provision of assistive technology for use in employment or education or broader policyand laws. Population disability data is essential for monitoring th quality and outcomes of policies for persons with disabilities. In particular, these data help to identify policy outcomes that maximize the participation of persons with disabilities in all areas of social life from transportation and communication, to participation in community life. Finally, with complete and reliable disabilitystatistics, state agencies will have the tools for assessing the cost- effectiveness of policies for persons with disabilities, which in turn can provide the evidence to persuade governments of their ultimate benefit for all citizens.

The National Policy for Persons with Disabilities (2006) recognizes that Persons with Disabilities are valuable human resource for the country and seeks to create an environment that provides equal opportunities, protection of their rights and fullparticipation in society. To facilitate the national objective, there is a need for collection, compilation and analysis of data on disability.

A number of International commitments and guidelines came into effect in the recent past targeting the welfare of the disabled persons. India is a signatory to the 'Declaration on the Full Participation and Equality of People with Disabilities in the Asia Pacific Region' (2000). India has ratified the 'UN Convention on the rights of Persons with Disabilities' (2008). India is also a signatory tothe 'Biwako Millennium Framework '(2002) for action towards an inclusive, barrier free and rights based society.

The 'Biwako Plus Five (2007): further efforts towards an inclusive, barrier-free and rights-based society for persons with disabilities in Asia and the Pacific' added the emphasis. The Incheon Strategy to "Make the Right Real" for Persons with Disabilities in Asia and the Pacific (2012) provides the Asian and Pacific region and the world with the first set of regionally agreed disability inclusive development Goals. The Incheon strategy will enable to track progress towards improving the quality of life, and   the fulfilment of the rights, of the region's persons with disability. The Sustainable Development Goals (2015) pledges for 'leaving no one behind'. Recognizing that the dignity of the human being is fundamental, the SDGs wish to see the Goals and targets met for allnations and peoples and for all segments of society and to endeavour to reach the furthest behind first.

The implementation and monitoring of these internationalcommitments demand sound database of disabled persons. Issues in measuring disability Some of the important issues being faced while developing a strong disability statistics are as follows:

DEFINING DISABILITY:
The definition of the population with disabilities is a key element in the design of a data collection activity, for it sets the scope and coverage of the whole data collection process. From the conceptual point of view, there is no universal definition of what constitutes a disability or of who should be considered as having a disability. Moreover, there is no one static condition of disability.

A disability is a result of the interaction between a person with a health condition and a particular environmental context. Individuals with similar health conditions may not be similarly disabled or share the same perception of their disability, depending on their environmental adaptations. For example, having access to technicalaids, services or medication, or physical adaptation to the environment may allow individuals to overcome their disabling conditions Disability is not an all-or nothing phenomenon but involves degrees of difficulty, limitation or dependence, ranging from slight to severe. Questions should be designed to capture those with severe as well as those with less severe forms of disabling conditions and should take into account any assistive devices or accommodations that the person may have. Coverage: Different purposes require different disability data. Eliciting information:

In places where disability is a stigma, people may be reluctant to report it. Also, this being a very sensitive question, the investigators need to be adequately trained to collect data on disabilities. The design of questions to identify persons in the population with disabilities presents complex problems. But efforts   are to be madeto design the questionnaire in such a manner that, all the target population could be correctly identified. Emerging data requirementsin the context of recent international commitments Incheon Strategyto "Make the Right Real" for Persons with Disabilities in Asia and⬚ the Pacific The Governments of the ESCAP region gathered in Incheon, Republic of Korea, from   29 October to 2 November 2012 to chart the course of the new Asian and Pacific Decade of Persons with Disabilities for the period 2013 to 2022 and adopted the Inchoen strategy which comprises 10 goals, 27 targets and 62 indicators.The Incheon strategy builds on the Convention on the Rights of Persons with Disabilities (CRPD) and the Biwako Millennium Framework for Action and Biwako Plus Five towards an Inclusive, Barrier – free and Rights - based Society for Persons with Disabilities in Asia and the Pacific. This will enable the region to track the progress towards improving the quality of life, and the fulfilment of the rights of the region' persons with disabilities. Goal 8 of the Incheon strategy specifically aims to 'Improve the reliability and comparability of disability data'.

MEASURING DISABILITY IN INDIA
The UN convention on the Persons with disabilities and its Optional Protocol was adopted on 13 December, 2006 at the United Nations Headquarters in New York. The Convention came into effect on 3 May, 2008. The Convention is intended as a human rights instrument with an explicit, social development dimension. It adopts a broad categorisation of persons with disabilities

and reaffirms that all persons with all types of disabilities must enjoy all human rights and fundamental freedoms.

It clarifies and qualifies how all categories of rights apply to persons with disabilities and identifies areas where adaptations have to be made for persons with disabilities to effectively exercise their rights and areas where their rights have been violated, and where protection of rights must be reinforced.

The purpose of the UN Convention on the Rights of Persons with Disabilities (UN CRPD) is to promote, defend and reinforce the human rights of all persons with disabilities. International Classification of Functioning, Disability and   Health (ICF) The International Classification of Functioning, Disability and Health, known more commonly as ICF, provide a standard language and framework for the description of health and health-related states. Like the first version published by the World Health Organization for trial purposes in 1980, ICF is a multipurpose classification intended for a wide range of uses I different sectors. It is a classification of health and health-related domains -- domains that help us to describe changes in body function and structure, what a person with a health condition can do in a standard environment (their level of capacity), as well as what they actually do in their usual environment (their level of performance).

SAMPLE SURVEYS ON DISABILITY BY NSSO

National Sample Survey Office (NSSO), made its first attempt to collect
information on the number of physically handicapped in its 15th round (July 1959- June 1960) which was confined to rural areas only. In NSSO 16th round (July 1960 – June 1961) the coverage was extended to urban areas. The subject was again taken up for nationwide survey in its 24th round (July 1969- June 1970) and 28th round (October 1973-   June 1974). The physical handicaps covered in the above mentioned surveys were not always same and information was collected through survey schedules meant for other subjects. First comprehensive survey in NSS 36th round (July- Dec 1981) followed by a survey in 47th round (July- December 1991) to cover all persons with one or more of the three physical disabilities – visual, communication (ie. Hearing and or speech) and locomotor. The lastsurvey was carried out by NSS in its 58th round (July- December 2002), which extended the coverage by mental disability in addition to the three physical disabilities (visual, communication an locomotor). Along with the particulars of physical and mental disabilities, the socio economic characteristics of the disabled such as their age, literacy, employment, vocational training etc were collected.

SOCIOCULTURAL BIASES AND DISCRIMINATION

The presence and persistence of sociocultural biases and discriminatory attitudes and practices can be readily identified as major contributors to vulnerability. Bias and discrimination are in a sense acts of social exclusion, as they prevent the groups that are the victims of those acts from fully participating in and benefiting from the wealth, power, knowledge and decision-making capacities of the larger society.

At their worst, socio-economic biases and discrimination can produce feelings of disempowerment, hopelessness and despair forthe future, further exacerbating vulnerability among the excluded groups. The inability to provide input to important policy decisions leaves them powerless and voiceless, resulting in their legitimate interests not being protected. Consequently, national policies and development programmes do not necessarily benefit those that are disenfranchised.

Still, worse, their interests may even be sacrificed in the pursuit of such policies and programmes. As a result, social groups, households and individuals subject to such misperception and discrimination experience greater vulnerability to social exclusion. 206. The following are presented below as illustrations of the negative effects of bias and discrimination: the images and misperceptions of older persons; the vulnerabilities experienced by migrants; discrimination against the disabled; groups particularly a risk in situations of conflict; and the lack of respect for traditional knowledge and cultures of indigenous persons.

IMAGES AND MISPERCEPTIONS OF OLDER PERSONS

On one level, perceptions of older persons follow the trajectory of a society's culture, religion, language, history and level of development. On another, they follow social conventions   that adhere to established precedents and, once rooted, are difficult to alter. The social convention of classifying people on the basis   oftheir age has enduring consequences that can create significant barriers to access and participation. are critical and active partners in families and societies through the care they provide to family members who might otherwise require more formal treatment; through the care and education they provide to children whose parents cannot afford childcare or who migrate elsewhere for work; through the countless other forms of volunteer work that they perform in communities and institutions everywhere; and through their help in conflict resolution and the rebuilding of communities following emergencies. In addition, older persons possess traditional knowledge and overall survival strategiesaccumulated over a lifetime of experience.

Paradoxically, however, older persons are cast in distorted images that inflate their physical and mental deterioration and dependence. The outcome is an anachronistic message that, on the   broaderlevel, colours an entire phase of life. It obscures older persons' contributions and generates ageism, discrimination and exclusion and, ultimately, contributes to a loss of

rights in the social, economicand political spheres. Routine media misrepresentation that idolizes youth and views ageing as a time of incapacity and stagnation is particularly damaging to older persons,
who already suffer greater exclusion, especially in an era of rapid technological change in which authority is often passed to younger members of society. Significantly, such images are not lost on centres of influence and power, such as employers, donors and policy makers — decision makers who can have an impact on older persons' access to structures and resources and therefore mitigate or increase vulnerability

Globalization of the media has contributed to spreading ageism to societies in which it was traditionally unknown. The forces of globalization that have ushered in consumerism and individualism in developing countries have compounded the devaluation of the status of older persons, encouraging the view that they are burdens and a financial drain. The effects are becoming visible far beyond the local level, with a lack of opportunities for older persons, combined with the absence of economic assets and added responsibilities owing to the outmigration of younger adults,conspiring to force on older persons into greater economic and social dependence.
Negative self-image is inextricably bound up with stereotypes and isanother factor that leads to social exclusion. Older persons with strong tendencies towards a negative self-image are also those whoare in the greatest need of support. Those in poverty and conflict show a marked decline in self-esteem as they age and tend   toshare a view of ageing as a time of worthlessness, incapacity and loss of status that leads to dependence. For many, fears and self doubt accumulate to such an extent that what is feared — exclusionand greater physical and economic dependence — becomes more likely. Low self-esteem becomes a risk in itself and helps to fosteran image of a population with whom no one, including older personsthemselves, wants to identify.

The perpetuation of misperceptions of ageing has a political impact as well. The expression "intergenerational conflict", which has appeared in the public discourse, suggests that, if steps are not taken, individual old-age pension and health-care security, or worse,national or even global financial stability, may be threatened with disruption. Such messages suggest a need to assign responsibility and ultimately serve as a pretext for cutting back on old-age provisions. Perceptions that an ageing society will deepen social conflict, however, are not so rooted in prejudices as to hold any particular age group responsible. Rather, social, economic and politically uncertain environments, with the support of the media, are shaping attitudes about society's unpreparedness to adjust to a changed demographic structure that has no precedent   and therefore no previous basis from which to proceed.

Women and men move through the ageing process in   differentways and encounter different obstacles and relative disadvantages en route. For women, balancing work and family responsibilities canbe all-consuming. Their role as principal caregiver in the family oftenlingers into old age, when they care for their spouses and/or, in areas ravaged by poverty and disease, including HIV/AIDS, for theirgrandchildren and other family members who are orphaned or sick.

MIGRANTS' VULNERABILITIES
Migration is a pervasive issue that has a bearing on the economy, the social fabric and the political life of many countries. Viewpoint on migration are polarized to the degree that it is difficult to hold a rational debate on the issue. Against such a background of contention, the human dimension of international migration   has often been missing from the policy agenda, and many migrants have increasingly found themselves vulnerable

First, in the course of the migration process, individuals lose the security of essential family-, community- and nation-based support structures, including traditional institutions that regulate power, decision-making and protection, while at the same time they are exposed to a host of hazards for which they are largely unprepared. To a significant extent, the vulnerability of migrants stems from the nature of the immigration process, which remains, in much of the world — apart from a handful of traditional countries of immigration — long, challenging and poorly organized. During thecourse of the immigration process, migrants often receive little assistance from the host country and end up relying on immigrant communities and immigration networks of questionable legitimacy.In trying to circumvent admissions delays and restrictions, an increasing number of migrants are putting themselves at risk by electing to be smuggled.

STIGMA
Stigma is when someone views you in a negative way because you have a distinguishing characteristic or personal trait that's thought tobe, or actually is, a disadvantage (a negative stereotype). Unfortunately, negative attitudes and beliefs toward people whohave a mental health condition are common.

Stigma can lead to discrimination. Discrimination may be obvious and direct, such as someone making a negative remark about your mental illness or your treatment. Or it may be unintentional or subtle, such as someone avoiding you because the person assumes you could be unstable, violent or dangerous due to your mental illness. You may even judge yourself.

Some of the harmful effects of stigma can include:

- Reluctance to seek help or treatment
- Lack of understanding by family, friends, co-workers or others
- Fewer opportunities for work, school or social activities ortrouble finding housing
- Bullying, physical violence or harassment
- Health insurance that doesn't adequately cover your mentalillness treatment
- The belief that you'll never succeed at certain challenges orthat you can't improve your situation

STEPS TO COPE WITH STIGMA

Here are some ways you can deal with stigma:

- Get treatment. You may be reluctant to admit you need treatment. Don't let the fear of being labeled with a mental illness prevent you from seeking help. Treatment can provide relief by identifying what's wrong and reducing symptoms that interfere with your work and personal life.
- Don't let stigma create self-doubt and shame. Stigma doesn't just come from others. You may mistakenly believe that your condition is a sign of personal weakness or that you should be able to control it without help. Seeking counseling, educating yourself about your condition and connecting with others who have mental illness can help you gain self-esteem and overcome destructive self-judgment.
- Don't isolate yourself. If you have a mental illness, you may be reluctant to tell anyone about it. Your family, friends, clergy or members of your community can offer you support if they know about your mental illness. Reach out to people you trust for the compassion, support and understanding you need.
- Don't equate yourself with your illness. You are not an illness. So instead of saying "I'm bipolar," say "I have bipolar disorder." Instead of calling yourself "a schizophrenic," say "I have schizophrenia."
- Join a support group. Some local and national groups, such as the National Alliance on Mental Illness (NAMI), offer local programs and internet resources that help reduce stigma by educating people who have mental illness, their families and the general public. Some state and federal agencies and programs, such as those that focus on vocational rehabilitation and the Department of Veterans Affairs (VA), offer support for people with mental illness.
- Get help at school. If you or your child has a mental illness that affects learning, find out what plans and programs might help. Discrimination against students because of a mental illness is against the law, and educators at primary, secondary and college levels are required to accommodate students as best they can. Talk to teachers, professors or administrators about the best approach and resources. If a teacher doesn' know about a student's disability, it can lead to discrimination, barriers to learning and poor grades.
- Speak out against stigma. Consider expressing your opinions at events, in letters to the editor or on the internet. It can help instill courage in others facing similar challenges and educate the public about mental illness.

Others' judgments almost always stem from a lack of understandingrather than information based on facts. Learning to accept your condition and recognize what you need to do to treat it, seeking support, and helping educate others can make a big difference.

SOCIAL DETERMINANTS OF CHILD ABUSE

Globally, child abuse (or child maltreatment) is a significant public health problem extending beyond culture, social context and race. Child abuse consists of any acts of commission or omissionby a parent, caregiver or other adult resulting in harm, potential for, or threat of harm to a child (0-18 years of age) even if the harm is unintentional. The World Health Organization (WHO) estimates that40 million children aged 0-14 years globally suffer from abuse and neglect that require health and social care.

The extent and trend of national or global rates, and determinants of child abuse are largely unknown. Studies in Egypt are sparse, estimating that 37% of children in Egypt suffer physical punishment with varying degrees of severity; 5 these acts of punishment, presumably committed as acts of child discipline, are engendered by a culture that places a high premium on child obedience and the positive effects of discipline

Social determinants of health (SDH) are conditions in which people are born, grow, live, work and age, including the health system. These conditions provide the freedom people need to live lives they value, and are shaped by the distribution of money, powerand resources at global, national and local levels. SDH that perpetuate child abuse can be avoided by reasonable societal level action; however, that they are not avoided indicates that they are unfair, unnecessary, unjust, and therefore inequitable. Givenchildren's need for safe, healthy, nurturing, and responsive living environments, the SDH that perpetuate child abuse are numerous, and need to be examined to understand the association between child abuse and intimate partner violence (IPV).

Children exposed to child abuse are often exposed to co-occurring domestic violence (DV) and environmental stressors. Households frequently experiencing IPV are commonly poor, undergo marital problems, life stressors, and other negative aspects of family life, including low parental education, unemployment,   insufficient income, and substance abuse. Other factors associated with increased risk for child abuse include young child age, minority status, and parental stress, immigrant families, single-parent families, stepfamilies, families with three or more children, children 0 - 3 years old, female sex, and older adolescence. Perpetrator- related risk factors such as parental mental health, chronic illness, criminal history, alcohol or drug abuse, and parental skills have alsobeen implicated with child abuse and IPV.

Knowledge of how the social determinants of child abuse operate and interact is an important first step towards developing interventions and policy-level change needed to improve the lives ofaffected children and families. To assess for associations, the following hypotheses were tested

Hypothesis I: The risk of experiencing child abuse will be higher forchildren exposed to domestic violence, even after controlling for potential confounders;

Hypothesis II: Mothers with tolerant attitudes towards wife beating will be more likely to abuse their child than those who do nottolerate wife beating;

Hypothesis III: Women exposed to generational IPV i.e. who had witnessed domestic violence in childhood, will be more likely to perpetrating child abuse, compared to those who were not so exposed; and

Hypothesis IV: Children in families of higher socio-economic position (SEP), as indicated by educational level of respondent or partner, and household wealth index, will be at lower risk of experiencing abuse compared to those of lower SEP.

The aim of this study was two-fold:
1 to determine the prevalence of child abuse in Egypt; and
2 to investigate factors associated with maternal abuse as socialdeterminants of child abuse.

DOMESTIC VIOLENCE

Domestic violence (also called intimate partner violence (IPV), domestic abuse or relationship abuse) is a pattern of behaviorsused by one partner to maintain power and control   over another partner in an intimate relationship.

Domestic violence does not discriminate. Anyone of any race, age, sexual orientation, religion or gender can be a victim – or perpetrator – of domestic violence. It can happen to people who are married, living together or who are dating. It affects people of all socioeconomic backgrounds and education levels.

Domestic violence includes behaviors that physically harm, arouse fear, prevent a partner from doing what they wish or force them to behave in ways they do not want. It includes the use of physical andsexual violence, threats and intimidation, emotional abuse and economic deprivation. Many of these different forms of domestic violence/abuse can be occurring at any one time within the same intimate relationship.

Think of the wheel as a diagram of the tactics an abusive partner uses to keep their victim in the relationship. While the inside of the wheel is comprised of subtle, continual behaviors, the outer ring represents   physical, visible violence. These are the abusive acts that are more overt and forceful, and often the intense acts that reinforce the regular use of other more subtle methods of abuse.

Although this Power & Control Wheel uses she/her pronouns for the victim and assumes a male perpetrator, abuse can happen to people of any gender in any type of relationship.

IT'S NOT ALWAYS EASY TO TELL AT THE BEGINNING OF A RELATIONSHIP IF ITWILL BECOME ABUSIVE.

In fact, many abusive partners may seem absolutely perfect in the early stages of a relationship. Possessive and controlling behaviors don't always appear overnight, but rather emerge and intensify as the relationship grows.

Domestic violence doesn't look the same in every relationship because every relationship is different. But one thing most abusive relationships have in common is that the abusive partner does manydifferent kinds of things to have more power and control over their partner.

Some of the signs of an abusive relationship include a partner who:
- Tells you that you can never do anything right
- Shows extreme jealousy of your friends and time spent away
- Keeps you or discourages you from seeing friends or familymembers
- Insults, demeans or shames you with put-downs
- Controls every penny spent in the household
- Takes your money or refuses to give you money for necessaryexpenses
- Looks at you or acts in ways that scare you
- Controls who you see, where you go, or what you do
- Prevents you from making your own decisions
- Tells you that you are a bad parent or threatens to harm ortake away your childre
- Prevents you from working or attending school
- Destroys your property or threatens to hurt or kill your pets
- Intimidates you with guns, knives or other weapons
- Pressures you to have sex when you don't want to or do thingssexually you're not comfortable with
- Pressures you to use drugs or alcohol

Explore the tabs below to learn some of the common warning signs of each type of abuse. Experiencing even one or two of thesebehaviors in a relationship is a red flag that abuse may be present. Remember, each type of abuse is serious, and no one deserves to experience abuse of any kind, for any reason. If you have concerns about what's happening in your relationship, contact us. We're here to listen and support you!

PHYSICAL ABUSE
You may be experiencing physical abuse if your partner has done or repeatedly does any of the following tactics of abuse:
- Pulling your hair, punching, slapping, kicking, biting orchoking you
- Forbidding you from eating or sleeping
- Hurting you with weapons
- Preventing you from calling the police or seeking medicalattention
- Harming your children Abandoning you in unfamiliar place
- Driving recklessly or dangerously when you are in the carwith them
- Forcing you to use drugs or alcohol (especially if you'vehad a substance abuse problem in the past)

Abuse DefinedYou are here:
(1) Home /
(2) Is This Abuse? /
(3) Abuse Defined

What Is Domestic Violence?
DOMESTIC VIOLENCE (ALSO CALLED INTIMATE PARTNER VIOLENCE (IPV), DOMESTIC ABUSE OR RELATIONSHIP ABUSE) IS A PATTERN OF BEHAVIORSUSED BY ONE PARTNER TO MAINTAIN POWER AND CONTROL OVER ANOTHER PARTNER IN AN INTIMATE RELATIONSHIP.

Domestic violence does not discriminate. Anyone of any race, age, sexual orientation, religion or gender can be a victim – or perpetrator – of domestic violence. It can happen to people who are married, living together or who are dating. It affects people of all socioeconomic backgrounds and education levels.

Domestic violence includes behaviors that physically harm, arouse fear, prevent a partner from doing what they wish or force them to behave in ways they do not want. It includes the use of physical andsexual violence, threats and intimidation, emotional abuse an economic deprivation. Many of these different forms of domestic violence/abuse can be occurring at any one time within the same intimate relationship.

Here at The Hotline, we use the **Power & Control Wheel*** to describe most accurately what occurs in an abusive relationship.

Think of the wheel as a diagram of the tactics an abusive partner uses to keep their victim in the relationship. While the inside of the wheel is comprised of subtle, continual behaviors, the outer ring represents   physical, visible violence. These are the abusive acts that are more overt and forceful, and often the intense acts that reinforce the regular use of other more subtle methods of abuse.

Although this Power & Control Wheel uses she/her pronouns forthe victim and assumes a male perpetrator, abuse can happen to people of any gender in any type of relationship Click image to enlarge Copyright by the Domestic Abuse Intervention Project 202 East Superior Street, Duluth, MN, 55802218-722-2781

Warning Signs of Domestic Violence

EMOTIONAL ABUSE
You may be in an emotionally/verbally abusive relationship ifyou partner exerts control through:

i. Calling you names, insulting you or continually criticizingyou

ii. Refusing to trust you and acting jealous or possessive

iii. Trying to isolate you from family or friends

iv. Monitoring where you go, who you call and who youspend time with

v. Demanding to know where you are every minute

vi. Trapping you in your home or preventing you fromleaving Using weapons to threaten to hurt you

vii. Punishing you by withholding affection

viii. Threatening to hurt you, the children, your family or yourpets

ix. Damaging your property when they're angry (throwingobjects, punching walls, kicking doors, etc.)

x. Humiliating you in any way

xi. Blaming you for the abuse

xii. Gaslighting

xiii. Accusing you of cheating and being often jealous of youroutside relationships

xiv. Serially cheating on you and then blaming you for his orher behavior

xv. Cheating on you intentionally to hurt you and thenthreatening to cheat again

xvi. Cheating to prove that they are more desired, worthy, etc.than you are

xvii. Attempting to control your appearance: what you wear,how much/little makeup you wear, etc.

xviii. Telling you that you will never find anyone better, or thatyou are lucky to be with a person like them

SEXUALLY ABUSIVE METHODS OF RETAINING POWER AND CONTROLINCLUDE AN ABUSIVE PARTNER:

- Forcing you to dress in a sexual way Insulting you in sexual ways or calls you sexual name
- Forcing or manipulating you into to having sex or performing sexual acts
- Holding you down during sex
- Demanding sex when you're sick, tired or after hurting you
- Hurting you with weapons or objects during sex
- Involving other people in sexual activities with you against yourwill
- Ignoring your feelings regarding sex
- Forcing you to watch pornography
- Purposefully trying to pass   on a sexually transmitted disease to you

SEXUAL COERCION

Sexual coercion lies on the 'continuum' of sexually aggressive behavior. It can vary from being egged on and persuaded, to being forced to have contact. It can be verbal and emotional, in the form ofstatements that make you feel pressure, guilt, or shame. You can also be made to feel forced through more subtle actions. For example, an abusive partner:

- Making you feel like you owe them — ex. Because you're in a relationship, because you've had sex before, because they spent money on you or bought you a gift
- Giving you drugs and alcohol to "loosen up" your inhibitions Playing on the fact that you're in a relationship, saying things such as: "Sex is the way to prove your love for me," "If I don't get sex from you I'll get it somewhere else
- Reacting negatively with sadness, anger or resentment if you say no or don't immediately agree to something
- Continuing to pressure you after you say no
- Making you feel threatened or afraid of what might happen if you say no
- Trying to normalize their sexual expectations: ex. "I need it, I'ma man"

Even if your partner isn't forcing you to do sexual acts against your will, being made to feel obligated is coercion in itself. Dating someone, being in a relationship, or being married never   means that you owe your partner intimacy of any kind.

REPRODUCTIVE COERCION IS A FORM OF POWER AND CONTROL WHERE ONE PARTNER STRIPS THE OTHER OF THE ABILITY TO CONTROL THEIR OWN REPRODUCTIVE SYSTEM. IT IS SOMETIMES DIFFICULT TO IDENTIFY THIS COERCION BECAUSE OTHER FORMS OF ABUSE ARE OFTEN OCCURRING SIMULTANEOUSLY.

Reproductive coercion can be exerted in many ways:

- Refusing to use a condom or other type of birth control
- Breaking or removing a condom during intercourse
- Lying about their methods of birth control (ex. lying abouthaving a vasectomy, lying about being on the pill)
- Refusing to "pull out" if that is the agreed upon method of birth control
- Forcing you to not use any birth control (ex. the pill, condom, shot, ring, etc.
- Removing birth control methods (ex. rings, IUDs, contraceptivepatches)
- Sabotaging birth control methods (ex. poking holes incondoms, tampering with pills or flushing them down the toilet)
- Withholding finances needed to purchase birth control
- Monitoring your menstrual cycles
- Forcing pregnancy and not supporting your decision aboutwhen or if you want to have a child
- Forcing you to get an abortion, or preventing you from gettingone
- Threatening you or acting violent if you don't comply with theirwishes to either end or continue a pregnancy
- Continually keeping you pregnant (getting you pregnant againshortly after you give birth)

Reproductive coercion can also come in the form of pressure, guilt and shame from an abusive partner. Some examples are if your abusive partner is constantly talking about having children or making you feel guilty for not having or wanting children with them especially if you already have kids with someone else.

ECONOMIC OR FINANCIAL ABUSE IS WHEN AN ABUSIVE PARTNER EXTENDS THEIR POWER AND CONTROL INTO THE AREA OF FINANCES. THIS ABUSE CAN TAKE DIFFERENT FORMS, INCLUDING AN ABUSIVE PARTNER:

Giving an allowance and closely watching how you spend it ordemanding receipts for purchase

- Placing your paycheck in their bank account and denying you access to it
- Preventing you from viewing or having access to bank accounts
- Forbidding you to work or limiting the hours that you can work
- Maxing out credit cards in your name without permission or notpaying the bills on credit cards, which could ruin your credit score
- Stealing money from you or your family and friends
- Using funds from children's savings accounts without yourpermission
- Living in your home but refusing to work or contribute to the household
- Making you give them your tax returns or confiscating joint tax returns
- Refusing to give you money to pay for necessities/shared expenses like food, clothing, transportation, or medical care and medicine

DIGITAL ABUSE IS THE USE OF TECHNOLOGIES SUCH AS TEXTING AND SOCIAL NETWORKING TO BULLY, HARASS, STALK OR INTIMIDATE A PARTNER. OFTEN THIS BEHAVIOR IS A FORM OF VERBAL OR EMOTIONAL ABUSE PERPETRATED ONLINE. YOU MAY BE EXPERIENCING DIGITAL ABUSE IF YOUR PARTNER:

Tells you who you can or can't be friends with on Facebook and other sites

- Sends you negative, insulting or even threatening emails,Facebook messages, tweets, DMs or other messages online.
- Uses sites like Facebook, Twitter, foursquare and others tokeep constant tabs on you.
- Puts you down in their status updates.
- Sends you unwanted, explicit pictures and demands you sendsome in return.
- Pressures you to send explicit videos.
- Steals or insists on being given your passwords.
- Constantly texts you and makes you feel like you can't beseparated from your phone for fear that you will be punished.
- Looks through your phone frequently, checks up on yourpictures, texts and outgoing calls.
- Tags you unkindly in pictures on Instagram, Tumblr, etc.
- Uses any kind of technology (such spyware or GPS in a car oron a phone) to monitor you. You never deserve to be mistreated, online or off. Remember:
- Your partner should respect your relationship boundaries.
- It is ok to turn off your phone. You have the right to be alone and spend time with friends and family without your partner getting angry. You do not have to text any pictures or statements that you areuncomfortable sending, especially nude or partially nude photos, known as "sexting.
- You lose control of any electronic message once your partner receives it. They may forward it, so don't send anything you fear could be seen by others.
- You do not have to share your passwords with anyone.
- Know your privacy settings. Social networks such as Facebookallow the user to control how their information is shared and who has access to it. These are often customizable and are found in the privacy section of the site. Remember, registering for some applications (apps) require you to change your privacy settings.
- Be mindful when using check-ins like Facebook Places and foursquare. Letting an abusive partner know where you are could be dangerous. Also, always ask your friends if it's ok for you to check them in. You never know if they are trying to keeptheir location secret.
- You have the right to feel comfortable and safe in your relationship, even online.

WHAT IS PEACE PSYCHOLOGY: VIOLENCE, NON-VIOLENCE, CONFLICT RESOLUTION AT MACRO LEVEL, ROLE OF MEDIA IN CONFLICT RESOLUTION?

Peace psychology

Peace psychology, area of specialization in the study of psychology that seeks to develop theory and practices that prevent violence and conflict and mitigate the effects they have on society. It also seeks to study and develop viable methods of promoting peace.

The roots of peace psychology are often traced to WilliamJames and a speech he gave at Stanford University in 1906. With World War I on the horizon, James talked about his belief that war satisfies a deeply felt human need for virtues such as loyalty, discipline, conformity, group cohesiveness, and duty. Healso observed that individuals who belong to a group, whether military or otherwise, experience a boost in self-pride when they are proud of their group. Most important, he argued that war is not likelyto be eliminated until humans have created a "moral equivalent of war," such as public service that allows people to experience the virtues that were associated with war making.

Many other psychologists and philosophers wrote about thepsychology of peace. A partial list includes Alfred Adler, Gordon Allport, Jeremy Bentham, James McKeen Cattell, Mary Whiton Calkins, Sigmund Freud, William McDougall, Charles Osgood, Ivan Pavlov, and Edward Tolman. Even Pythagoras would qualify, because of his writings on nonviolence and appreciation for the more-insidious form of violence called structural violence, which killspeople slowly by depriving them of basic need satisfaction (e.g., poverty).

A recurrent theme among peace psychologists has been that war is built, not born, and the related idea that war is biologically possible but not inevitable. Those ideas are captured in a numbe
of manifestos issued by psychologists. One statement was signedby almost 4,000 psychologists after World War II. Another, the Seville Statement, was issued in 1986 by 20 highly respected scientists during the United Nations International Year of Peace. Because war is built or constructed, a great deal of research in peace psychology has sought to identify environmental conditions that are linked to violence and peaceful behaviour.

Peace psychology was given a significant boost during the ColdWar (c. mid-1940s through the early 1990s), when the conflict between the United States and Soviet Union heated up and thethreat of nuclear annihilation seemed imminent, leading psychologists to create concepts to better understand intergroup conflict and its resolution. Also important was the establishment of the 48th division of the American Psychological Association, called Peace Psychology, in 1990. Shortly thereafter, a journal was established, Peace and Conflict: Journal of Peace Psychology. Since then, doctoral-level training programs in peace psychology have been established around the world.
Peace psychology is now global in scope. It recognizes that violence can be cultural, which occurs when beliefs are used to justify either direct or structural violence. Direct violence injures or kills people quickly and dramatically, whereas structural violence is much more widespread and kills far more people by depriving them of satisfaction of their basic needs. For example, when people starve even though there's enough food for everyone, the distribution system is creating structural violence. If a person justifies the deaths of starving people by blaming them for their situation (called blaming the victim), that person is engagingin cultural violence. Direct violence is supported by the culturally violent notion of just war theory, which argues that under certain conditions, it is acceptable to kill others (e.g., defense of the homeland, using war as a last resort). One of the main challenges for peace psychology is to deepen understanding of the structural and cultural roots of violence, a problem that is particularly important when security concerns revolve around the preventionof terrorism.

PSYCHOLOGY'S ROLE IN WORLD WAR I AND II

The concerns of peace psychologists are deeply rooted in the field of psychology, not only because the promotion of human well-being is central to the mission of psychology (APA By laws but also because psychologists have long been concerned about war and peace. William James, a founder of psychology in the United States, has been regarded as the first peace psychologist (Deutsch, 1995). Just prior to World War I, James gave an address on "the moral equivalent of war" in which he highlighted the enthusiastic readiness of humans to rally around the military flag (James, 1995), a social psychological phenomena akin to "nationalism" that has played out repeatedly for generations, especially when relationsbetween nations become hostile. James argued that militaristic urges are deeply rooted in humans and that societies must learn to channel the satisfaction of their needs in productive directions. Psychologists did not follow James' advice, but they did become involved in U.S. military affairs during the First World War.

Among the more important contributions of psychologists to the war effort was the development of group intelligence tests that were used to select and classify new recruits, a development that "put psychology on the map" (Smith, 1986, p.24). Psychologists ha even greater involvement during the Second World War. A number of specialties in psychology emerged and supported the war effort. Clinical psychologists developed and administered tests to place personnel within the military establishment and they also treated war-related emotional problems. Social psychologists contributedtheir expertise, developing propaganda designed to promote the war effort by boosting morale at home and demoralizing the enemy abroad.

A number of psychologists worked with the Office of StrategicServices, the precursor of the Central Intelligence Agency, selectingand training people involved in "undercover" activities in Europe andthe Far East. Human factors psychologists participated in the designof weaponry and other instruments used by the military, and experimental psychologists trained nonhumans to perform human tasks.

The best-known example of the latter was B. F. Skinner's research in which he trained pigeons to guide pilotless missiles to targets, a program that was ultimately discarded (Herman, 1995). In all these activities, psychologists were enthusiastic participants in the effort towin World War II, a war that was regarded by most people as a just war.

PSYCHOLOGY'S ROLE IN THE COLD WAR

The ideology of Realpolitik has guided the conduct of foreign policy worldwide for nearly three centuries (Klare & Chandrani, 1998). Realpolitik is the belief that politics is reducible to three basic goals: keeping power, increasing power, and demonstrating power (Morganthau, 1972). The international politics of the United States was, and continues to be, primarily guided by the ideology of Realpolitik. From a Realpolitik perspective, one sees security in th international system as the balanced capacity among states to use coercive power. Furthermore, because it is assumed that all sovereign states seek to maximize their power, and they operate within an international structure that is anarchical, the best way to ensure security is to be militarily strong and to adopt a policy of deterrence. According to the logic of deterrence,   each state can best ensure its security by threatening any would-be aggressor with a retaliatory blow that would be unbearably costly to the aggressor. By the conclusion of World War II, a tidy bipolar superpower arrangement had emerged in the world. The United States and Soviet Union were locked into an adversarialrelationship in which they competed and concentrated theirresources in an arms race, a Cold War that resulted in enormous stockpiles of conventional and nuclear weapons. During the early years of the Cold War, psychologists continued to support the policies of the U.S. government.

Tensions between the United States and Soviet Union grew, as did the arsenals of nuclear weapons that were aimed at each other. There were scattered attempts by committees of the American Psychological Association (APA) and the Society for the Psychological Study of Social Issues (SPSSI) to analyze the implications of the new atomic warfare capability on future international relations, as well as the potential psychological effects on populations experiencing atomic bombardment. Generally, theseearly committees lacked focus but agreed that the major psychological concern was citizens' attitudes toward atomic warfare and energy. They "emphasized the need to accurately assess and control public opinion in order t achieve public consensus regarding foreign relations and atomic war" (Morawski & Goldstein, 1985, p. 278).

THE POST-COLD WAR ERA: PEACE PSYCHOLOGY COMES OF AGE THE COLD

War was a power struggle of global proportions that made certain categories of violence salient. Using the state as the focal unit of analysis, scholars concentrated their attention on interstate wars, wars of liberation, secessionist movements, civil wars, and wars in which the superpowers directly intervened militarily (i.e., interventionist wars). Although many other forms of violence were prevalent, from a state-centered perspective, what mattered most were those struggles that had a direct bearing on the strategic, U.S.–Soviet balance of power (George, 1983). Since the end of the Cold War in the late 1980s, the planet's bipolar superpower structure has reconfigured dramatically and entirely new categories of security concerns have emerged.

To be sure, the sovereign states of the international system will still have conflicts to manage, but increasingly, patterns of violence are not neatly following the contours of our inherited system of sovereign states. In the post–Cold War era, a complex pattern of interlacing schisms is emerging, which divides people not so much by state boundaries but by ethnicity, religion, economic well being, population density, and environmental sustainability (Klare, 1998).

A small sample of what we are now observing globally is the outbreak of ethnic violence and other forms of identity group conflictand violence, a growing number of economic and political refugees, ecological devastation and pockets of food insecurity, concentrations of drug-related violence, and international terrorism. These problems are within and across international boundaries an underscore the need to reorient peace psychology and enlarge its scope of practice. The current volume was conceived within the context of these new challenges and represents an attempt to reinvigorate the search for psychological analyses that can inform theory and practice in peace psychology for the twenty-first century.

ORGANIZATION OF THE BOOK: THE FOUR-WAY MODEL

Section I: Direct Violence The current volume retains the traditional focus of peace psychology on international relations by applying psychological concepts and theory to problems of   interstate violence and the threat of nuclear war. In addition, because direct violence does not neatly follow the contours of the sovereign state system, chapters in Section I reflect a wider radius of violent episodes that vary in scale from two-person intimate relations to the large-scale violence of genocide. While different in scale and complexity, these varied forms of violence share several features: They allengender direct, acute insults to the psychological or physical well- being of individuals or groups, 14 and they erupt periodically as events or episodes. The analytic tools of peace psychologists are central to understanding many forms of direct violence.   For instance, in Section I, many of the contributors from around the world underscore the importance of social identity processes, which are manifest when individuals begin   to identifywith particular groups and favor their ingroups over outgroups. Quitenaturally, the basic need to have a sense of who we are is inextricably woven into the fabric of our identity groups. Conflict and violence often erupts when two or more groups of individuals have different identities and see each other as threats their identity group's continued existence.

These identitybased conflicts are central to many forms of violence including hate crimes, gang violence, ethnic conflicts, and even genocide. Sovereign states have been woefully inadequate in dealing with identity-based problems. Also reflected throughout the text is peace psychologists' growing appreciation for the structural roots of violent episodes. For example, patriarchal structures inwhich males dominate females play a role in intimate violence. Similarly, cultural narratives that denigrate gays, lesbians, and other marginalized identity groups are predisposing conditions for direct violence. Section II looks closer at some forms of violence that are deeply rooted in the structures of a society, what we are calling "structural violence." Section II: Structural Violence Today, an increasing number of peace psychologists are concerned about structural violence (Galtung, 1969), an insidious form of violence that is built into the fabric of political and economic structures of a society (Christie, 1997; Pilisuk, 1998; Schwebel, 1997).

Structural violence is a problem in and of itself, killing people just as surely as direct violence. But structural vio- 15 lence kills people slowly by depriving them of satisfying their basic needs. Life spans are curtailed when people are socially dominated, politically oppressed, or economically exploited.

Structural violence is a global problem in scope, reflected in vast disparities in wealth and health, both within and between societies. Section II examines a number of forms of structural violence, all of which engender structure-based inequalities in the production, allocation, andutilization of material and non-material resources. Galtung (1969) proposed that one way to define structural violence was to calculatethe number of avoidable deaths. For instance, if people die from exposure to inclement conditions when shelter is available for them somewhere in the world, then structural violence is taking place. Similarly, structural violence occurs when death is caused by scarcities in food, inadequatenutrition, lack of health care, and other forms of deprivation that could be redressed if distribution systems were more equitably structured. The chapters in Section II make it clear that structural violence is endemic to economic systems that produce a concentration of wealth for some while exploiting others, political systems that give access to some and oppress others, and hierarchical social systems that are suffused with ethnocentrism and intolerance.

CONFLICT RESOLUTION AND MANAGEMENT: THE MACRO PERSPECTIVE

Conflicts arise from the pursuit of divergent interests, goals and aspirations by individuals or groups in a defined social and physical environment. According to changes in the social environment such as contestable accessto new political positions or perceptions of new resources arising from development in the physical environment are fertile grounds for conflicts involving individuals and groups, who are interested inusing the new resources to achieve their goals. The past ten to fifteen years were characterized by the occurrence of some of the most violent conflicts among several ethnic and religious communities in different regions and states of Nigeria. As in hardly was any region spared some of these conflicts, even though the conflicts differed either in prevalence and intensity, or their protracted or nonprotracted nature. By definition, it implies that conflict is natural to human nature. That is, all humans or groups of humans have goals and interests which may be different with the goals and interests of other groups.

This makes conflict inevitable. Change is a natural phenomenon that produces the major social forces that shape societies. When these changes occur, especially at the middle and micro levels where their effects are individually or personally experienced, they do not happen quickly but are gradual in altering the ecological order, the system of stratification and the social institutions of an entire society causing societies to undergo industrial, political and urban revolution leaving in its wake social problems such as politica and economic exclusion of some groups, injustice, poverty,exploitation, diseases, inequality etc.

These conditions places some people or   group at an advantage over others and the inability of the social structures in   place to bridge this gap and where possible reduce the disparity can cause frustrations and acts of aggression from the disadvantaged individuals or groups.

Where these shows of frustration and aggression are ignored and not nipped at the bud, they most often are excuses to violently play out the hostility towards the exploitative group or groups and may escalate to become larger than the small groups or individualsinvolved to include an entire ethnic groups or organizations.

OVERVIEW OF CONFLICT

Conflict is an inevitable phenomenon in this universe. As long as humankind exists, there must be conflict. Conflict has   been variously defined by different authors but it is technically seen as an opposition among social entities directed against each other [3]. Similarly, [4] sees conflict as a political process that generates from diversity of choices and distribution of scarce resources in the society.[5] further adds that the occurrence of cheat and aggressive behavior on the part of individuals or groups that lead to the frustration of others may cause conflict. Also [6] states that conflict is the struggle over values or claims to states, power and scarce resources which the aims of the group or individuals involvedare not only to obtain the desired values but are to neutralize, injure or eliminate rivals. Thus, conflict is present when two or more parties perceive that their interests are incompatible, express hostile attitudes, or take, pursu their interests through actions that damage the other parties. These parties may be individuals, small or large groups, and countries. From the foregone, it can be deduced that opposition is the order of contrast to cooperation. Meaning that wherever and whenever cooperation and understanding is lacking opposition sets in.

Therefore, conflict can be explained to be an adversarial relationship involving at least two individuals or collective actors over a range or series of issues such as resources control, power, status, values, goals interest etc. Conflict is a social situation in which at least two parties are involved who strive for goals, makingit goal oriented or directed activity designed to improve the position of one party at the expense of the other.

It is a perceived state of incompatibility between two or more people or groups and among values where the achievement of one value can be realized only at the expense of the other values. Conflict is an escalated competition between two or more parties each of which aims to gain advantage of some kind and at least oneof the parties believes that the conflict is over a set of mutually incompatible goals. Conflicts may or may not be expressed in behaviours. It is one of the energies of life and thus common,natural and unavoidable but its pattern of expression can make or mar any relationship.

3. CONCEPT OF MACRO

Conflict When individuals or groups who had previously been latent over their grievances, oppressions, deprivation, injustices etc suddenly or gradually begin to express these feelings through certain obnoxious behaviours in order to call for attention to their situation which escalates to an entire group, ethnic, state or even national and international, macro conflict has occurred. Macro leve conflicts are expression of existing adversary's relationships through aggressive behaviours as a result of unresolved incompatible interest in the social structure of the system or organization. These lapses in the structural functionalism of a society make it difficult for the rules and status that exists to provide social control or social order which is necessary for survival.

Macro conflicts are open or external expression of dissatisfaction of the aggrieved group which is aimed at injuring the other party or reducing it if not totally eliminating the existing relationship between both groups. Conflict that has degenerated to macro level becomes difficult and complex for the parties involved to personally resolve their differences alone without the aid of external assistance. Most times the aggrieved parties may not even be able to state the immediate or direct cause of conflict as they usually lose track of theoriginal causes of grievance.

Again, conflicts can escalate to its macro level as a result of the presence of indirect or secondary parties to the conflict. These groups of persons or organizations complicate conflict situations and are difficult to identify because their involvements are by proxy through provisions of war aid and weapons, financial support etc.

They are known as "shadow" parties in conflict. Macro conflicts focus on the broader impacts or effects of conflict or its lack thereof.It considers a wider aspect in conflict such as an entire society, age group or age bracket, population groups, countries, economies,social class etc. Macro conflict goes beyond an individual or organization and conflict at the macro level changes social stratification, economic power and diplomatic stance of a society and thereby its future.

Causes of Macro Conflict Resources

Conflicts can emerge due to resources. These conflicts arise when two or more groups aspire for the same scarce resources andwhere the aspiring parties demanding for these resources are more than the available scarce resources. The desire for control of the available scarce resources by a privileged group to the disadvantage of the other aspirants can cause conflicts e.g. the Niger Delta Region crises in Nigeria. Values: Conflicts may arise due to differences in the value of the people or organization. Values here include philosophy, ideologies, religions etc.

The value a group of people or ethnic nationality places on another group may be a constant cause for conflict especially where these values or perceptions are discriminatory and undermines the other group thereby limiting the prospects in certain areas of their lives or hindering their access to certain self actualizing opportunities. Values can bring about oppressive and unequal social structures. e.g Fulani Cattle Herdsmen and some indigent communities in Northern Nigeria, the Igbo cast system.

MACRO CONFLICT RESOLUTION AND MANAGEMENT

Conflict at the macro level has most often gone beyond the controlof the conflicting parties, so even when they see the need for peace,may require the presence and assistance of a third party to initiate the peace move. The third party usually provides neutral groundthat are safe enough for peace talk and unbiased opinions forconflicting parties to consider and upon which their decision can be based. Also, warring or conflicting groups may want to enter into peace talks through representative bodies who are expected to, if possible find lasting solution to the existing strives Conflict resolution is seen by [10] as a variety of approaches aimed at terminating conflict through the constructive solving of problem while conflict management is defined as the process of reducing thenegative and destructive capacity of conflict through a number of measures and by working with and through the parties involved in the conflict. For the purpose of this paper, conflict resolution and management is defined as constructive processes or procedures adopted for solving problems which are aimed at terminating conflicts or reducing its negative anddestructive effects by working with and through the conflicting parties.

This means that some conflicts can be permanently resolved when the basic needs of the parties have been met with all necessary satisfiers and their fears allayed and there are non-resolvable conflicts and these can be transformed, regulated or managed e.g. values. Management of conflicts covers the entire handling of conflict positively through its different stages, including efforts made towards prevention by being proactive, conflict limitation,containment and litigation.

CONCLUSION

Conflicts are natural phenomenon in human society. Depending on their intensity, conflicts are expressed sometimes in violent or non- violent ways. They are social situations in which at least two parties with incompatible goals strive to achieve these goals at the expenseof each other. Conflicts occur at all levels of human interaction Macro conflicts focus on the broader impacts of conflict on entire groups or social strata.

The causes of conflict are varied and includes resources, values, oppressive social order, mismanagement of information etc. and these could be permanently resolved but where this is impossible will be managed through collaboration, alternative dispute desolation (ADR), negotiation, conciliation, mediation, arbitration,adjudication, crisis management and multi-track approach methods.Conflict is an inevitable occurrence in every human existence, at all levels and takes different forms which could be either violent or non-violent ways.

THE ROLE OF THE MEDIA IN PEACE BUILDING, CONFLICT MANAGEMENT, AND PREVENTION

Information is power and insight can impact on public discourse. This way, perceptions can be changed by access to media. Different types of media are utilised globally to distribute knowledge and idealistically, free mass media is a tool of and signpost for democracy. Freedom of expression is not only the core of a healthy media but also a fundamental human right and vital for a democraticstructure. It stands for freedom of speech, the right to information and the representation of different opinions in a heterogeneoussociety. In any culture of prevention, effective and democratic mediaare an essential part and indispensable for societies trying to makea transition towards peace and democracy. Harry S. Truman once said "You can never get all the facts from just one newspaper, and unless you have all the facts, you cannot make proper judgements about what is going on this statement reflects the need for free access to unbiased information. Not giving people the possibility of political participation and not allowing them to express themselves freely is a significant cause of conflict. On the one hand free, independent and pluralistic media provide a platform for debate and different opinions. On the other hand, media can be misused for propaganda purposes, to incite hatred and spread rumours and therefore artificially create tensions.

The transmission of ideas is also not limited to conventional media such as newspapers, TV or radio.

Lack of information can, at any stage of a conflict, make people desperate, restless and easy to manipulate. The ability to make informed decisions strengthens societies and fosters economic growth, democratic structures and the positive outlook on the future.For this very reason, the United Nations Millennium Declaration stressed the need "to ensure the freedom of the media to perform their essential role and the right of the public to have access to information.

Journalism does not need justification for its existence. Its service tosociety is justification in itself. Journalism can not only help to distribute information but also counter hate-speech and create an environment of balanced opinions, an information equilibrium]. For the media it can be problematic to find a balance between preventing harm caused by speech and protecting individual expression. Being able to find this balance, however is important especially in conflict situations. Responsible journalism does not justre-publish press releases but is truly concerned with a truthful,balanced and fair account of events. In order to achieve this journalists have to stay clear of judgemental representations and describe reality without embellishment]. If democracy is to work properly, society needs access to news and information; analysis o the status quo, debate, practical information and exchange as well as entertainment are needed and provided by the media. The definition of conflict and defining conflict areas is not easy and no two places are alike. Journalists need to know what they can expecton sight in order to define the objectives of their project.

In case of a crisis or a conflict, the international media can attract worldwide attention. The mass media is a pervasive part of daily life especially in industrialised countries and thus able to shine a light on conflicts anywhere in the world. Since most armed   conflictsthese days have governmental and not territorial reasons; the parties are often concerned with making sure that the majority of people are on "their" side, which bears a lot of potential for misrepresenting facts and trying to seize control over the distributionof information. For this very reason the intervention of unbiased andfree global media is important not only for the world public but also for the people directly affected. The number of conflicts, however, that gets international attention is small; therefore local media   is vital in this context.

Broadcasting news by using community radios can help reach people in different areas, even with different languages more easily.This way people can be addressed directly and their own personal experiences and lives can be incorporated much better, than with foreign media. The danger of manipulation and inflammation ofethnic tensions, however, cannot be ignored. Another advantage of local media, especially radio is that in border areas it is possible to convey peace messages to passing fighters and refugees alike]. Democratic media structures need more than this; it is vital that the use of information within a society is not solemnly passive but that the population gets actively involved in creating content and broadcasting it.

WHAT IS WELLBEING AND SELF-GROWTH: TYPES OF WELLBEING [HEDONIC AND EUDEMONIC], CHARACTER STRENGTHS, RESILIENCE AND POST-TRAUMATIC GROWTH?

WELLBEING

Well-being is the experience of health, happiness, and prosperity. It includes having good mental health, high life satisfaction, a sense ofmeaning or purpose, and ability to manage stress. More generally, well-being is just feeling well (Take this quiz to discover your level ofwell-being.) Well-being is something sought by just about everyone, because it includes so many positive things — feeling happy, healthy, socially connected, and purposeful. Unfortunately, well-being appears to be in decline, at least in the U.S. And increasing your well-being can betough without knowing what to do and how to do it.

These are some of the reasons why I founded The Berkeley Well- Being Institute — an organization that translates the science of well-being into simple tools and products that help you build your well- being. And they are the reasons why I wrote Outsmart Your Smartphone: Conscious Tech Habits for Finding Happiness, Balance, and Connection IRL, which helps people tackle new challenges that interfere with our well-being in the technology age.

Can You Actually Improve Your Well-Being
Increasing your well-being is simple; there are tons of skills you can build. But increasing your well-being is not always   easy: Figuring out what parts of well-being are most important for you and figuring out how, exactly, to build well-being skills usually require some extra help.

How Long Does It Take to Improve Well-Being?
Usually when people start consistently using science-based techniques for enhancing well-being, they begin to feel better quickly. In the studies I've conducted and read, most people show significant improvements within five weeks.

But you have to stick to it. If you are feeling better after five weeks, you can't just stop there.
Why? Well, you probably already know that if you stop eating healthy and go back to eating junk food, then you'll end up back where you started. It turns out that the exact same thing is true for different types of well-being. If you want to maintain the benefits yougain, you'll have to continue to engage in well-being-boosting practices to maintain your skills. So it's really helpful to have strategies   and   tools   that   help   you   stick   to   your well-being goals — for example, a happiness and well-being plan or a well-being boosting activity that you can continue to use throughout your life.

Here's what you need to know:

Where Does Well-Being Come From?
Well-being emerges from your thoughts, actions, and experiences most of which you have control over. For example, when wethink positive, we tend to have greater emotional well-being. When we pursue meaningful relationships, we tend to have better social well-being. And when we lose our job — or just hate it — we tend tohave lower workplace well-being. These examples start to reveal how broad well-being is, and how many different types of well-beingthere are Because well-being is such a broad experience, let's break it down into its different types.

5 MAJOR TYPES OF WELL-BEING
- Emotional Well-Being. The ability to practice stress- management techniques, be resilient, and generate theemotions that lead to good feelings.
- Physical Well-Being. The ability to improve the functioning of your body through healthy eating and good exercise habits.

- Social Well-Being. The ability to communicate, develop meaningful relationships with others, and maintain a support network that helps you overcome loneliness.
- Workplace Well-Being. The ability to pursue your interests, values, and purpose in order to gain meaning, happiness, and enrichment professionally.
- Societal Well-Being. The ability to actively participate in a thriving community, culture, and environment.

To build your overall well-being, you have to make sure all of these types are functioning to an extent.

Think of it like this: Imagine you are in a car. Your engine works great, and maybe your transmission works pretty well, too, but your brakes don't work. Because your brakes don't work, it doesn't reall
matter how well your engine works; you're still going to have trouble going about your life.
The same is true for your well-being. If everything else in your life is going great, but you feel lonely, or you're eating unhealthfully, other areas of your life will be affected, and you likely won't feel as well asyou want to.

Because each part of well-being is important to your overall sense of well-being, let's talk about how to build each type of well-being:

Emotional Well-Being. To develop emotional well-being, we need to build emotional skills — skills like positive thinking, emotion regulation, and mindfulness, for example. Often, we need to build a variety of these skills to cope with the wide variety of situations we encounter in our lives. When we have built these emotional well- being skills, we can better cope with stress, handle our emotions in the face of challenges, and quickly recover from   disappointments. As a result, we can enjoy our lives a bit more, be   happier and pursue our goals a bit more effectively.

Here are some of the skills that research suggests contribute to emotional well-being:
- Happiness Skills
- Mindfulness Skills
- Positive Thinking Skills
- Resilience Skills

Physical Well-Being. To develop our physical well-being, we need toknow what a healthy diet and exercise routine looks like, so that we can implement effective strategies in our daily lives. When w improve our physical well-being, not only do we feel better, our newfound health can also help prevent many diseases, heal our guts, boost our emotional well-being, and limit the Bnumber of health challenges we have to deal with in our lives.

Here are some of the things that can help you boost your physical well-being:
- Eating for Health
- Detoxing Your Body
- Correcting Nutritional Deficiencies
- Removing Plastic From Your Home

Unfortunately, it's possible to eat healthy but still be unhealthy. We can accidentally miss important foods or nutrients. Or we can overburden ourselves with toxins from plastic or processed food. Asa result, we may need to eat additional foods, detox our bodies, or prevent these toxins from entering our bodies again. This is why it's essential to learn about health, so that we can make the right changes — those that lead to long-term health and well-being.

Social Well-Being. To develop social well-being, we need to build our social skills, like gratitude, kindness, and communication. Socialskills make it easier for us to have positive interactions with others, helping us to feel less lonely, angry, or disconnected. When we have developed our social well-being, we feel more meaningfully connected to others.

Here are some of the skills that research suggests contribute to better social well-being:
- Practicing Gratitud
- Building Meaningful Social Connections
- Managing Your Relationship with Technology

It's important to know that building social well-being is one the best ways to build emotional well-being. When we feel socially connected, we also tend to just feel better, have more positiveemotions, and we are able to cope better with challenges. This is why it's essential to build our social well-being.

Workplace Well-Being. To develop our workplace well-being, weneed to build skills that help us pursue what really matters to us. This can include building professional skills which help us to advance more effectively, but it also includes things like living our values and maintaining work-life balance. These skills let us enjoy our work more, helping us to stay focused, motivated, and successful at work. When we have developed workplace well-being,our work, and therefore each day, feels more fulfilling.

Here are some of the key skills you need for workplace well-being:
- Maintaining Work-Life Balance
- Finding Your Purpose

Because we spend so much time at work, building our workplace well-being has a big impact on our overall well-being.

Societal Well-Being. To develop societal well-being, we need   tobuild skills that make us feel interconnected with all things. We needto know how to support our environment, build stronger local communities, and foster a culture of compassion, fairness, and kindness. These skills help us feel like we're part of a thriving community that really supports one another and the world a large. When we cultivate societal well-being, we feel like we are a part of something bigger than just ourselves and live happily.

Although each of us only makes up a tiny fraction of a society, it takes all of us to create societal well-being. If each of us   did one kind act for someone else in our community, then we would live in a very kind community. Or if all of us decide we are going to recycle, then suddenly we create a world with significantly less waste. In order to live in a healthy society, we too need to contribute tomaking a healthy society.

Here are some of the skills you can build for greater societal well- being:
- Living Your Values
- Creating a Plastic-Free Home
- Making Positive Impacts in Other People's Lives
- Kindness

Who Benefits Most from Building Well-Being?
Not everyone experiences the same benefits from building their well-being. For example, lots of research suggests that the more motivated you are to build well-being skills, the greater the impact. Perhaps this is not surprising.

Still other research shows that having skills like a growth mindset or a positive attitude can actually help you build your other well-being skills more easily. This is why I tend to encourage people to build these skills first — afterward, you may be able to increase the other types of well-being more easily In addition, building well-being skills is perhaps most beneficial for people struggling the most, particularly if they've recently undergonesomething stressful. It may be harder to build well-being during this time, but the impact may be greater, because there is more room forimprovement.

There Is No Magic About Building Well-Being
Keep in mind, it takes time and effort to build any new skill set — that includes well-being skills. It's important to be realistic with yourself about what you can reasonably accomplish in a given amount of time. Having unrealistic expectations can lead you to giveup before you've reached your well-being goals. So it's key to createa realistic plan for your well-being, stick to it, and take small actions every day that add up to big improvements up over time.

If you've read my earlier posts, you might know that I too have struggled with aspects of my well-being, particularly with maintaining work-life balance. The truth is, we all struggle, and new struggles can and will pop up, even if you're doing well. But the longer we've worked on strengthening our well-being skills, the easier it is to be resilient, take the actions needed to bounce back, and continue moving forward.

Growing your well-being is a lifelong pursuit, but it is totally worth it.

HEDONIC AND EUDAIMONIC WELL-BEING
Hedonic versus Eudaimonic Conceptions   of Well-being: Evidence of Differential Associations with Self-reported Well-being Conceptions of well-being are individuals' cognitive representations of the nature and experience of well-being. Numerous professiona thinkers from a broad range of disciplines have theorized about the nature of well-being and "the good life", providing explicit conceptualizations of the experience of well-being. Contemporary psychological research has also begun to examine how laypersons conceptualize and think about the nature of well-being (e.g., King and Napa 1998; McMahan and Estes

2010; Ng et al. 2003), often focusing on the degree to which individuals define well-being in hedonic (e.g., the experience of pleasure) and eudaimonic (e.g., theexperience of meaning) terms.

As a fundamental representation of wellness, these conceptions likely exert a pervasive influence on behavior and psychological functioning. In two studies, the above research is extended by investigating the relative effects of both hedonic and eudaimonic dimensions of individual conceptions of well-being on several aspects of experienced well-being.

Formal and Lay Conceptions of Well-being Well-being refers tooptimal functioning and experience (Ryan and Deci 2001). The precise nature of optimal functioning is not necessarily clear, however, and many philosophers and psychologists   provide differing conceptions of well-being. Although numerous and sometimes complex, these conceptions tend to revolve around two distinct, but related philosophies:
1. hedonism and
2. eudaimonism

A hedonic view of well-being equates wellbeing with pleasure and happiness (Kahneman et al. 1999; Ryan and Deci 2001). Alternatively, a eudaimonic view of well-being conceptualizes well- being in terms of the cultivation of personal strengths   an contribution to the greater good (Aristotle, trans. 2000), acting in accordance with one's inner nature and deeply held values (Waterman 1993), the realization of one's true potential (Ryff and Keyes 1995), and the experience of purpose or meaning in life (Ryff 1989). Hedonic and eudaimonic approaches   to well-being can be further distinguished by the degree to which they rely on subjective versus objective criteria for determining wellness.

To illustrate, determinations of wellness from the hedonic approach center around the experience of pleasure, a subjectively-determinedpositive affective state. From a eudaimonic perspective, well-beingis achieved by meeting objectively-valid needs which are suggestedto be rooted in human nature and whose realization is conducive to human growth (Fromm 1947). In short, the hedonic approach focuses on subjectively-determined positive mental states, whereas the eudaimonic approach focuses on experiences that are objectively good for the person (Kagan 1992).

Contemporary research within psychology further indicates that laypeople may also hold conceptions of well-being that are similar tothose advocated by professionals (e.g., King and Napa 1998; McMahan and Estes 2010; Ng et al. 2003; Pflug 2009; Tseng 2007).For example, research has found that lay conceptions of well-being incorporate both hedonic and eudaimonic aspects (King and Napa 1998), and individuals differ in the degree to which they conceptualize well-being in hedonic and eudaimonic terms (McMahan and Estes 2010).

Additionally, pleasure and meaning are consistently included in individuals' conceptions   of wellbeing, but highly valued items that are theoretically not considered to be definitive of well-being, suc as material wealth, are typically not included (King and Napa 1998; Tseng 2007). In general, laypersons' conceptions of   well-being seem to mirror the conceptions of well-being provided by philosophers and psychologists, and laypeople seem to similarly differ in terms of the degree to which they advocate a more hedonic or eudaimonic definition of well-being.

HEDONIC VERSUS EUDAIMONIC APPROACHES TO WELL-BEING

The degree to which individuals define well-being in hedonic and eudaimonic terms has large practical implications and likely influences behavior in several domains of functioning, particularly those relevant to the experience of well-being (Ryan and Deci 2001). Implicit in theorizing on hedonic versus eudaimonic approaches to well-being is the assumption that these approaches are differently associated with positive psychological functioning. Specifically, eudaimonic theories maintain that many desiredoutcomes   which are pleasurable may not necessarily be good for the individual and would thus not promote wellness (Ryan and Deci 2001).

To illustrate, dining at a fine restaurant and running a marathon mayyield experiences of a similar hedonic quality, such as the experience of enjoyment and pleasure. However, running amarathon likely provides more opportunity for personal growth, self- development, and feelings of competency than dining at fine restaurant and would thus likely yield increased well-being. Additionally, eudaimonic approaches to well-being, because they involve activities that are inherently good for the individual, are likely associated with long-term and enduring well- being, whereas the sense of well-being derived from the experienceof simple pleasures likely dissipates in the short-term (Steger et al 2008). In support, research indicates that physical pleasure is associated with life satisfaction in the short-term (i.e., within a day), but not in the long-term (i.e., over several weeks) (Oishi et al. 2001).Further, the positive effects of eudaimonic activity during a single day are associated with subsequent reports of well-being over several days (Steger et al. 2008).

PERSONALLY-EXPRESSIVE ACTIVITIES

(Waterman 2005; Waterman et al. 2008), and psychological well- being (Ryff 1989; Ryff and Singer 1998), have found that behaviors and cognition indicative of a eudaimonic approach are generally associated with positive psychological functioning. Research also indicates that in some cases, behaviors and cognition indicative of a hedonic approach may actually be detrimental to well-being. For example, sensation-seeking has been associated with a number of negative outcomes, including substance use (Carrol and Zuckerman1977; Zuckerman 1994) and risky behaviors (Zuckerman 2009).

Although a great deal of research has documented the positiveeffects of eudaimonic activities, less research has examined the relative impact of both hedonic and eudaimonic approaches on well-being. Existing empirical research suggests, however, that eudaimonic approaches may be relatively more important for well- being than hedonic approaches. For example, daily eudaimonicactivity was found to be more robustly associated with well-being than behaviors aimed at experiencing pleasure or obtaining materialgoods (Steger et al. 2008). Similarly, orientation to happiness, a construct measuring the degree to which individuals attempt to achieve happiness through   pleasure, meaning, or engagement, has been found to be positively associated with life satisfaction (Peterson et al. 2005). Specifically orientations to meaning and to engagement, representing eudaimonic approaches to well-being, have been found to be more robustly associated with life satisfaction than an orientation to pleasure in both national (e.g., Peterson et al. 2005) and cross- national studies (Park et al. 2009). Further, lay conceptions of well- being have been found to be associated with multiple self-report indicators of well-being, including satisfaction with life, vitality, positive affect, and meaning in life, with eudaimonic dimensions indicating more numerous and generally stronger associations with wellbeing than hedonic dimensions (McMahan and Estes 2010).

CHARACTER STRENGTHS

Character Strengths and Virtues is a groundbreaking handbookcompiling the work of **researchers** to create a classification system for widely valued positive traits.

This handbook also intends to provide an empirical theoretical framework that will assist positive psychology practitioners in developing practical applications for the field.

There are 6 classes of virtues that are made up of 24 character strengths:
- **Wisdom** and Knowledge
- Courage Humanit
- Justice
- Temperance
- Transcendence

Researchers approached the measurement of "good character" based on the strengths of authenticity, persistence, kindness, gratitude, hope, humor, and more.

Before you read on, we thought you might like to **download our 3 Positive Psychology Exercises for free.** These science-based exercises will explore fundamental aspects of positive psychology including strengths, values and self-compassion and will give you the tools to enhance the wellbeing of your clients, students or employees.

Cultures around the world have valued the study of human strength and virtue. Psychologists have a particular interest in it as they workto encourage individuals to develop these traits. While all cultures value human virtues, different cultures express or act on virtues in different ways based on differing societal values and norms.

Martin Seligman and his colleagues studied all major religions and philosophical traditions and found that the same six virtues (i.e. courage, humanity, justice, etc.) were shared in virtually all cultures across three millennia.

Since these virtues are considered too abstract to be studied scientifically, positive psychology practitioners focused   their attention on the strengths of character created by virtues, and created tools for their measurement.

The main assessment instruments they used to measure thosestrengths were
- Structured interviews
- Questionnaires
- Informant Reports
- Behavioral Experiments
- Observations

The main criteria for characters strengths that they came   up withare that each trait should:

- Be stable across time and situations
- Be valued in its own right, even in the absence of otherbenefits
- Be recognized and valued in almost every culture, beconsidered non-controversial and independent of politics.
- Cultures provide role models that possess the trait so otherpeople can recognize its worth.
- Parents aim to instil the trait or value in their children.

THE CSV HANDBOOK'S LIST

The Handbook delves into each of these six traits. We've summarized key points here.

• VIRTUE OF WISDOM AND KNOWLEDGE

The more curious and creative we allow ourselves to become, the more we gain perspective and wisdom and will, in turn, love whatwe are learning. This is developing the virtue of wisdom and knowledge Strengths that accompany this virtue involve acquiring and using knowledge:

- Creativity (e.g. Albert Einstein's creativity led him to acquire knowledge and wisdom about the universe)
- Curiosity
- Open-mindedness
- Love of Learning
- Perspective and Wisdom (Fun fact: many studies have found that adults' self-ratings of perspective and wisdom do not depend on age, which contrasts the popular idea that ourwisdom increases with age).

• VIRTUE OF COURAGE

The braver and more persistent we become, the more our integrity will increase because we will reach a state of feeling vital, and this results in being more courageous in character.

Strengths that accompany this virtue involve accomplishing goals in the face of things that oppose it:

- Bravery
- Persistence
- Integrity
- Vitality

• VIRTUE OF HUMANITY

There is a reason why Oprah Winfrey is seen as a symbol of virtue for humanitarians: on every show, she approaches her guests wit respect, appreciation, and interest (social intelligence), she practices kindness through her charity work, and she shows her love to her friends and family.

Strengths that accompany this virtue include caring and befriending others:

- Love
- Kindness
- Social intelligence

• VIRTUE OF JUSTICE

Mahatma Gandhi was the leader of the Indian independence movement in British-ruled India. He led India to independence and helped created movements for civil rights and freedom by being an active citizen in nonviolent disobedience. His work has been appliedworldwide for its universality.

Strengths that accompany this virtue include those that build ahealthy and stable community:

- Being an active citizen who is socially responsible, loyal, and ateam member.
- Fairness
- Leadership

• VIRTUE OF TEMPERANCE

Being forgiving, merciful, humble, prudent, and in control of our behaviors and instincts prevents us from being arrogant, selfish, or any other trait that is excessive or unbalanced Strengths that are included in this virtue are those that protectagainst excess:

- Forgiveness and mercy
- Humility and modesty
- Prudence
- Self-Regulation and Self-control

• VIRTUE OF TRANSCENDENCE

The Dalai Lama is a transcendent being who speaks openly why he never loses hope in humanity's potential. He also appreciates nature in its perfection and lives according to what he believes is hisintended purpose.

Strengths that accompany this virtue include those that forge connections to the larger universe and provide meaning:
* Appreciation of beauty and excellence
* Gratitude
* Hope
* Humor and playfulness
* **Spirituality**, or a sense of purpose

POSITIVE PSYCHOLOGY & CHARACTER STRENGTHS AND VIRTUES

Positive psychology practitioners can count on practical applicationsto help individuals and organizations identify their strengths and usethem to increase and maintain their levels of well-being They also emphasize that these character strengths exist on acontinuum; positive traits are regarded as individual differences that exist in degrees rather than all-or-nothing categories.

In fact, the handbook has an internal subtitle entitled "A Manual of the Sanities" because it is intended to do for psychological well- being what the DSM does for psychological disorders: to add systematic knowledge and ways to master new skills and topics.

Research shows that these human strengths can act as buffers against mental illness. For instance, being optimistic prevents one's chances of becoming depressed. The absence of particularstrengths may be an indication of psychopathology. Positive psychology therapists, counselors, coaches, and   other psychological professions use these new methods   and techniques to help build people's strength and broaden their lives.

It should be noted that many researchers are advocating grouping these 24 traits into just four classes of strength (Intellectual, Social, Temperance, and Transcendence) or even three classes (excludingtranscendence), as evidence has shown that these classes do an adequate job of capturing all 24 original traits.

Others caution that people occasionally use these traits to excess, which can become a liability to the person. For example, some people may use humor as a defense mechanism in order to avoid dealing with a tragedy or coma.

WHAT STRENGTHS DO WOMEN SCORE HIGHER?

There's an interest in identifying dominant character strengths in genders and how it is developed As Martin Seligman and his colleagues studied all major religions and philosophical traditions to find universal virtues, much of the research on gender and character strengths have been cross- cultural also.

In a study by Brdar, Anic, & Rijavec on gender differences and character strengths, women scored highest on the strengths of honesty, kindness, love, gratitude, and fairness.

Life satisfaction for women was predicted by zest, gratitude, hope, appreciation of beauty/excellence, and love for other women. Arecent study by Mann showed that women tend to score higher on gratitude than men. Alex Linley and colleagues reported in a UK study that women not only scored higher in interpersonal strengths, such as love and kindness, but on social intelligence, too.

In a cross-cultural study in Spain by Ovejero and Cardenal, they found that femininity was positively correlated with love, social intelligence, appreciation of beauty, love of learning, forgiveness, spirituality, and creativity. The more masculine a man was, the morehe correlated negatively with these character strengths.

WHAT STRENGTHS DO MEN SCORE HIGHER?

Brdar, Anic & Rijavac reported that men score highest on honesty, hope, humor, gratitude, and curiosity. Their life satisfaction was predicted by creativity, perspective, fairness, and humor. Alex Linley and colleagues study showed that men scored higher than females on creativity.

Miljković and Rijavec's study found sex differences in a sample of college students. Men not only scored higher in creativity, but als leadership, self-control, and zest. These findings are congruent withgender stereotypes, as the study by Ovejero and Cardenal in Spain showed that men did not equate typical masculine strengths with love, forgiveness, love of learning, and so on.

In a Croatian sample, Brdar and colleagues found that men viewed cognitive strengths as a greater predictor for life satisfaction.

Men saw strengths such as teamwork, **kindness**, perspective, and courage to be a stronger connection to life satisfaction than other strengths. There is an important limitation to this sample population,as most of the participants were women.

WHAT CAN WE LEARN FROM BOTH?

While there are differences in character strengths between men andwomen, there are many that they share. Both genders saw gratitude, hope, and zest as being related to higher life satisfaction, as well as the tendency to live in accordance with the strengths that are valued in their particular culture.

Studies confirm that there is a duality between genders, but only when both genders identify strongly with gender stereotypes. Itmakes one wonder if men and women are inherently born with certain strengths, or if the cultural influence of certain traits prioritizes different traits based on gender norms.

Development of Character Strengths in Children Peterson and Seligman's, Character Strengths in Action handbook (2004) theorized that it is not common for some young children to demonstrate gratitude, open-mindedness, authenticity, and forgiveness.

Park and Peterson's study (2006) confirmed this theoretical speculation, concluding that these sophisticated character strengthsusually require a degree of cognitive maturation that   develops during adolescence. So although gratitude is associated with happiness in adolescents and adulthood, this is not the case in young children.

Park and Peterson's study found that the association of gratitude with happiness starts at age seven "Gratitude is seen as a human strength that enhances one's personal and relational well-being and is beneficial for society as a whole." – Simmel

Although most young children are not yet cognitively mature enoughfor sophisticated character strengths, there are many fundamental character strengths that are developed at a very early stage.
The strengths of love, zest, and hope are associated with happinessstarting at a very young age. The strengths of love and hope are dependent on the infant and caregiver relationship. A secure attachment to the caregiver at infancy is more likely to result in psychological and social well adjustment throughout their lives.

The nurturing of a child plays a significant role in their development, and role modeling is an important way of teaching a child certain character strengths as they imitate behavior and can then embrace the strength as one of their own.

Most young children don't have the cognitive maturity to display gratitude but have the ability to display love and hope. Therefore, gratitude must not be expected from a young child but must be taught.

Positive education programs have been developed to help children and adolescents focus on character strengths. There are certain character strengths in adolescents that have a clearer impact on psychological well-being. These strengths must be fostered to ensure life long fulfillment and satisfaction.

"Character strengths are influenced by family, community, societal, and other contextual factors. At least in theory, character strengths are malleable; they can be taught and acquired through practice." – Gillham, et al

CHARACTER STRENGTHS AND WELL-BEING IN ADOLESCENTS

The majority of the research today on character strengths focuses on adults, despite the known importance of childhood and adolescence on character development.

Research into character strengths shows which promote positive development and prevent psychopathology.

Dahlsgaard, Park, and Peterson discovered that adolescents with higher levels of zest, hope, and leadership displayed lower levels of anxiety and depression in comparison to their peers with   lowerlevels of these strengths. Other research findings suggested that adolescent character strengths contribute to well-being (Gillham, et al, 2011).

The research suggests that transcendence (eg. gratitude, meaning, and hope) predicts life satisfaction, demonstrating the importance ofadolescents developing positive relationships, creating dreams, andfinding a sense of purpose.

VIA CHARACTER STRENGTHS YOUTH SURVEY

Parents, educators, and researchers have requested the VIA: institute on character strengths to develop a VIA survey that is especially aimed at youths. Take the **VIA psychometric data – youth survey** if you are between the ages of 10-17.

CONCLUSION

The measurement of character strengths and the different traits thatgo into making them have many applications, from life satisfaction to happiness and other well-being predictors. These measurement tools have been used to study how these strengths have beendeveloped across genders and age groups.

What strengths do you possess? What implications can you see thisresearch having in our world today? Can you see how it may apply to your own life?

Please share your thoughts in the comment section below. We hope you enjoyed reading this article. Don't forget to **download our 3 Positive Psychology Exercises for free**. If you wish for more, our **Positive Psychology Toolkit©** contains over 300 science-based positive psychology exercises, interventions, questionnaires and assessments for practitioners to use in their therapy, coaching or workplace.

RESILIENCE AND POST-TRAUMATIC GROWTH

Resilience: How we piece ourselves back together Resilience is a broad and complex concept that encompasses all the patterns of behavior which contribute to a person adapting to distressing life circumstances. Resilience is the ability to cope with negative emotions that arise from a stressful experience and function atnormal or close to normal capacity; resilience then is a demonstration of survival in the face of overwhelming life circumstances. A range of factors have beenidentified that are linked to resiliency—they encompass attributes of a person, such as being sociable, having a sense of humor and being hopeful; as well as social dimensions such as experiences of parental   warmth,nurturing in the family unit, support at school and success in at leastone area of life .

Resilience in a specific area of one's life does not guarantee resilience across all functional areas. Indeed, research into, and theories of resilience indicate that resilience in one area of life can co-exist with high risk behaviors, social and emotional withdrawal, and maladaptive survival tactics. Further experience of childhood trauma is associated with lower levels of resilience and PTG following a traumatic event in adulthood.

Yet, people who suffer trauma can be viewed as having enormous potential to survive and the survival tactics used must be seen as normal reactions to abnormal circumstances.

POST TRAUMATIC GROWTH:

Post Traumatic Growth (PTG) refers to positive changes that are experienced by an individual as a result of a struggle with highly challenging life circumstances .

The life circumstances must constitute a trauma, crisis, or highly stressful experience that challenges the way a person sees the world and their place in it. Experiences where one faces death, disabling injury, or significant loss of possessions may cause peopleto question what is meaningful in life. Research by Tedeschi and Calhoun in the area of PTG has contributed to our understanding of what constitutes PTG and what is needed to achieve it. The researchers identified five types of PTG (2)

- Greater appreciation for life, which may include a shift in priorities, seeing pleasure in things that were once taken for granted.

- Closer, more intimate relationships with others, characterized by increased compassion and empathy for others.
- Seeing new opportunities in life and setting new life goals. This often requires the person to let go of the possibilities and goals that were part of their life before the trauma.
- A sense of increased personal strength - recognizing that bad experiences happen, we are vulnerable, but survival is possible.
- Positive spiritual change such as greater affinity with one's faith and more engagement with the bigger questions about one's existence and humanity. It's important to keep in mind that growth does not occur as a direct consequence of the traumatic experience but in the aftermath of it and the struggle to find a new normal. Growth can, and usually does, happen during the same period of time that unpleasant psychological and emotional reactions are present. How does growth happen? Growth is considered to be both an outcome and a process.

Two main processes are involved in achieving growth:

EMOTIONAL PROCESSING:

In the time following a traumatic experience individuals are often consumed by overwhelming emotion which can be described as intrusive and distressing. Being aware of those emotions, having a willingness to feel the feelings and expressing/disclosing the emotions are critical to moving toward growth. When a person is able to identify those distressing emotions yet still be able t experience positive emotions, then growth from the experience is much more likely. Emotional processing then requires a level of literacy about emotions in order to engage in the   cognitive processes and to make meaning of the experience. This is often a lengthy process.

COGNITIVE PROCESSING

involves recognizing that life has changed and now must be restructured with a new identity. The traumatic experience becomespart of this new identity and a new life purpose is established. Resilience is required for growth to occur; you have to be able to survive the initial distress in order to achieve positive growth. Being resilient, however, does not necessarily ensure growth will happen.

WHAT IS HEALTH: HEALTH PROMOTING AND HEALTH COMPROMISING BEHAVIORS, LIFE STYLE AND CHRONIC DISEASES [DIABETES, HYPERTENSION, CORONARY HEARTDISEASE], PSYCHONEUROIMMUNOLOGY [CANCER, HIV/AIDS]?

HEALTH

Health psychology is a specialty area that focuses on how biology, psychology, behavior, and social factors influence health and illness. Other terms including medical psychology and behaviora medicine are sometimes used interchangeably with the term health psychology.

Health and illness are influenced by a wide variety of factors. While contagious and hereditary illness are   common, many behavioral and psychological factors can impact overall physical well-being andvarious medical conditions.

The field of health psychology is focused on promoting health aswell as the prevention and treatment of disease and illness. Health psychologists also focus on understanding how people react to,cope with, and recover from illness. Some health psychologistswork to improve the health care system and the government's approach to health care policy.

Illnesses Related to Psychological and Behavioral Factors
- Stroke
- Heart disease
- HIV/AIDS
- Cancer
- Birth defects and infant mortality
- Infectious diseases

Division 38 of the American Psychological Association is devoted to health psychology. According to the division, their focus is on a better understanding of health and illness, studying thepsychological factors that impact health, and contributing to the health care system and health policy.

The field of health psychology emerged in the 1970s to address the rapidly changing field of healthcare. Life expectancy was muchlower then, due to lack of basic sanitation and the prevalence of infectious diseases. Today, life expectancy in the U.S. is around 80 years, and the leading causes of mortality are chronic   diseasesoften linked to lifestyle.[2] Health psychology helps address thesechanges in health.

By looking at the patterns of behavior that underlie disease and death, health psychologists hope to help people live better, and healthier, lives.

How Is Health Psychology Unique?
Because health psychology emphasizes how behavior influences health, it is well positioned to help people change the behaviors thatcontribute to health and well-being. For example, psychologists whowork in this field might conduct applied research on how to prevent unhealthy behaviors such as smoking and look for new ways to encourage healthy actions such as exercising.

For example, while most people realize that eating a diet high in sugar is not good for their health, many people continue to engagein such behaviors regardless of the possible short-term and long- term consequences. Health psychologists look at the psychological factors that influence these health choices and explore ways to motivate people to make better health choices.[3]

The US Centers for Disease Control National Center for Health Statistics compiles data regarding death in the nation and   its causes. Congruent with data trends throughout this century, nearly half of all deaths in the United States can be linked to behaviors or other risk factors that are mostly preventable Specifically, in the most recent CDC report (2012), the rate of death has declined for all leading causes except suicide; life expectancy isat an all-time high (78.8 years); and yet every hour about 83 Americans die from   heart disease and stroke. More than a quarter of those deaths are preventable.

Cancer remained second; followed chronic lower respiratory diseases, primarily chronic obstructive pulmonary diseases (COPD) such as emphysema and chronic bronchitis; followed by drug poisonings including overdoses and then fatal falls among an increasingly elder population.)[4]
Current Issues in Health Psychology Health psychologists work with individuals, groups,   and communities to decrease risk factors, improve overall health, and reduce illness. They conduct research and provide services in areasincluding:

- Stress reduction
- Weight management
- Smoking cessation
- Improving daily nutrition
- Reducing risky sexual behaviors
- Hospice care and grief counseling
- Preventing illness
- Understanding the effects of illness
- Improving recovery

Teaching coping skill
The Biosocial Model in Health Psychology
Today, the main approach used in health psychology is known as the biosocial model. According to this view, illness and health are the results of a combination of biological, psychological, and social factors.[5]

- **Biological factors** include inherited personality traits andgenetic conditions.
- **Psychological factors** involve lifestyle, personalitycharacteristics, and stress levels.
- **Social factors** include such things as social support systems,family relationships, and cultural beliefs.

Health Psychology in Practice
Health psychology is a rapidly growing field. As increasing numbers of people seek to take control of their own health, more and more people are seeking health-related information and resources. Healthpsychologists are focused on educating people about their ownhealth and well-being, so they are perfectly suited to fill this rising demand.

Many health psychologists work specifically in the area of prevention, focusing on helping people stop health problems before they start.

This may include helping people maintain a healthy weight, avoid risky or unhealthy behaviors, and maintain a positive outlook that can combat stress, depression, and anxiety.
Another way that health psychologists can help is by educating and training other health professionals. By incorporating

knowledge fro health psychology, physicians, nurses, nutritionists, and other health practitioners can better incorporate psychological approaches into how they treat patients.

HEALTH PROMOTION

Health promotion is among the foremost concerns of modern society. As with many problems of considerable social significance, most health problems are caused by what people do and what people do not do. People eat too much, exercise too little, and visit healthcare providers too infrequently, among many other things.

Understanding and solving these problems is a task for the behavioral sciences, and applied behavior analysts have been addressing problems related to health and fitness since the earliest days of the field.

The primary focus of this chapter is on applied behavior analysis research related to health promotion through diet, exercise, and medication adherence, as addressing these issues would significantly improve health across many populations.

Health promotion is the process of enabling people and communities to increase control over factors that influence their health, and thereby to improve their health (adapted from the Ottawa Charter of Health Promotion, 1986; Box 2.7). Health promotion is a guiding concept involving activities intended to enhance individual and community health and well-being (Box 2.8). It seeks to increase involvement and control by the individual and the community in their own health. It acts to improve health and social welfare, and to reduce specific determinants of diseases and risk factors that adversely affect the health, well-being, and productive capacities of an individual or society, setting target based on the size of the problem but also the feasibility of successful intervention, in a cost-effective way. This can be through direct contact with the patient or risk group, or act indirectly through changes in the environment, legislation, or public policy. Control of AIDS relies on an array of interventions that promote change in sexual behavior and other contributory risks such as sharing of needles among drug users, screening of blood supply, safe hygienic practices in health care settings, and education of groups at risk such as teenagers, sex workers, migrant workers, and many others. Control of AIDS is also a clinical problem in that patients need antiretroviral therapy (ART), but this becomes a management and policy issue for making these drugs available and at an affordable price for the poor countries most affected. This is an example of the challenge and effectiveness of health promotion and the New Public Health.

HEALTH PROMOTION INTERVENTIONS

Health promotion interventions have also been shown to have beneficial effects on PCMDs. These interventions include developing skills to improve perinatal health, teaching women about infant development, engaging and stimulating infants, and encouraging sensitivity and responsiveness toward infants. These types of interventions aim to improve mother-infant interaction and maternal self-efficacy and satisfaction (Rahman et al., 2013) and often give women an opportunity to share concerns and feelings, and receive social support from a group (Clarke et al., 2013).

The systematic reviews of PCMD treatment reported that health promotion interventions brought about improvements in PCMDs compared with usual care but with smaller effect sizes than the psychological interventions (Clarke et al., 2013). These studie included those conducted by Cooper et al. (2002, 2009), Baker-Henningham, Powell, Walker, and Grantham-McGregor (2005), Rahman, Iqbal, Roberts, and Husain (2009), Tripathy et al. (2010), Morris et al. (2012), Langer et al. (1996), le Roux et al. (2013), Robledo-Colonia, Sandoval-Restrepo, Mosquera- Valderrama, Escobar-Hurtado, and Ramírez-Vélez (2012), and Aracena et al. (2009). Clarke et al. examined seven of these health promotion interventions and reported a pooled effect size of −0.15; (95% CI: −0.27 and −0.02) on PCMDs. This effect size is much smaller than for psychological interventions but still larger than for no treatment.

HEALTH PROMOTION IN SCHOOLS

Health promotion in schools is a topic of both practical and empirical interest. Schools which provide comprehensive school health promotion programs are more effective in encouraging children to adopt health-enhancing behaviors and reducing health-compromising behaviors than schools that provide health education alone. Quantitative reviews of prevention and intervention program targeting adolescent drug use, smoking, and alcohol consumption were presented.
Research into the effectiveness of comprehensive school health programs provides evidence of the positive influence that such programs can exert on student health behaviors. However, conditions that enable effective school health promotion programs to be initiated and maintained depend on several school organizational and program implementation factors.

These strategies are supported by five priority action areas as outlined in the Ottawa Charter for health promotion
•Build healthy public policy.
•Create supportive environments for health.
•Strengthen community action for health.
•Develop personal skills.

•Reorient health services.

- Address the population as a whole in health-related issues, ineveryday life as well as people at risk for specific diseases.
- Direct action to risk factors or causes of illness or death.
- 3.Undertake activist approach to seek out and remedy risk factors inthe community that adversely affect health.
- Promote factors that contribute to a better condition of health of thepopulation.
- Initiate actions against health hazards, including communication,education, legislation, fiscal measures, organizational change, community development, and spontaneous local activities.
- 6.Involve public participation in defining problems and deciding onaction.
- 7.Advocate relevant environmental, health, and social policy.
- 8.Encourage health professional participation in health education andhealth advocacy.
- 9.Advocate for health based on human rights and solidarity.
- 10.Invest in sustainable policies, actions, and infrastructure to addressthe determinants of health.
- 11.Build capacity for policy development, leadership, health promotionpractice, knowledge transfer and research, and health literacy.
- 12.Regulate and legislate to ensure a high level of protection from harm and enable equal opportunity for health and well-being for all people.
- 13.Partner and build alliances with public, private, non-governmental, and international organizations and civil society to create sustainable actions.
- 14. Make the promotion of health central to the global developmentagenda.

Salutogenesis

Health promotion is the process by which people increase theircontrol over the determinants of their own health, thereby improving health and quality of life. In this context, quality of life refers to the perception that one is capable of managing one's health and life, that one's needs are being met, and that one is not being denied opportunities to achieve happiness and life satisfaction, regardless of eventual health, social, or economic limitations (World Health Organization, 1986). This perspective calls for a model of health promotion that emphasizes the development of empowerment and itis coherent with Aaron Antonovsky's concept of salutogenesis inwhich individuals are responsible, active, and participative (Eriksson& Lindström, 2006).

The theory of salutogenesis, or the salutogenic model (Antonovsky, 1996), represents a paradigm change in health promotion because it focuses on the factors that facilitate or optimize health rather than on the treatment or prevention of diseases (ie, the pathogenic model). Antonovsky suggested that health promotion has been overly concerned with risk factors rather than attempting to understand how people move in the direction of health. The salutogenic approach underlines the need for people to understand the factors that actively promote health instead of concentratin efforts and resources on negative outcomes. Hence, the assets model attempts to synthesize evidence based on the combination offactors that protect or promote health, well-being, and achievement (Morgan & Ziglio, 2007).

Antonovsky (1996) developed his salutogenic model during the Second World War, trying to determine what helps people maintain health under dramatic situations and how they recover from such situations. He suggested that those who have more favorable biological, psychosocial, and material resources, so-called general life resources (eg, money, social capital, cultural capital, intelligence), are more successful in dealing with life's challenges and recovering from life's problems than those who have fewer suchresources (Rivera, Ramos, & Moreno, 2011).

Furthermore, Antonovsky (1996) referred to the importance of what he called the (internal) sense of coherence (SOC): a "generalized orientation towards the world, which perceives it, in a continuum, as comprehensible, manageable and meaningful" (p. 15). The SOC has three dimensions: the cognitive dimension or comprehensibility;the behavioral dimension or manageability, and the motivationaldimension or meaningfulness. The SOC is thought to facilitate movement toward health because it provides the individual with the sense that the world and life events are understandable, ordered, and even predictable (ie, comprehensibility), the belief that one has the necessary resources to cope and manage events (ie, manageability), and the belief that life's challenges are worthy of investment of effort and resources (ie, meaningfulness; Rivera, Garcia-Moya, Moreno, & Ramos, 2013).

Psychosocial correlates of health compromising the major causes of adolescent mortality are not diseases, but are primarily related to preventable social, environmental and behavioral factors (Irwin and Millstein, 1986; Millstein, 1989). The three primary causes of mortality during adolescence are injuries, homicide and suicide; together they are responsible for 75% of all adolescent deaths (Millstein et al, 1993).

Major sources of morbidity include injury and disability associated with the use of motor or recreational vehicles, pregnancy complications, sexually transmitted diseases and consequences of substance abuse (Millstein et al., 1993).

Among adolescent females, eating disorders are another significant source of morbidity, and the use of unhealthy weight loss methods may have numerous psychological and physical health consequences (Nylander, 1971; Pugliese et al., 1983; French and Jeffery, 1994; Neumark-Sztainer, 1995).

To improve adolescent health it is essential to reduce the frequency,delay the onset and aim towards the prevention of behaviors associated with morbidity and mortality among youth. Following the identification of health-compromising behaviors to be targeted for intervention, the next step in building effective prevention programs is to understand the factors associated with these behaviors among adolescents at different stages of development.

Numerous studies on health-compromising behaviors among adolescents indicate that these Social Cognitive Theory (SCT) discusses the importance of personal, socio-environmental and behavioral factors on behavior and the reciprocal relations between all of these factors (Bandura, 1977, 1986). SCT has particular relevance for explaining involvement in health-compromising behaviors among youth. Jessor has developed a model specifically aimed at explaining adolescent risk behavior/lifestyle which incorporates a number of principles similar to those in SCT (Jessor, 1991, 1992, 1993). Personal, socio-environmental and behavioral factors are shown to influence adolescent risk behavior with reciprocal relationships among all of the factors.

1). Personal factors include those from the psychological domain: self-esteem, emotional well-being and risk-taking disposition. Socioenvironmental factors include both actual and perceived components such as family structure and family connectedness, school connectedness, and stressful life experiences such as past physical and sexual abuse.

Behavioral factors include school achievement, involvement in extracurricular activities and attendance at religious services. It should be noted that the placement of these variables into these larger categories is not clearcut as most of these variables have personal, Health-compromising behaviors Unhealthy weight loss behaviorsRespondents indicated involvement in any of the following behaviors for weight control purposes: laxative use, water pills (diuretics), diet pills and vomiting. Internal consistency as measuredby Cronbach's a was 0.60. Scores ranged from 0 to 4, for thenumber of methods used.

SUBSTANCE ABUSE BEHAVIORS RESPONDENTS

indicated frequency and quantity of consumption for cigarettes, alcohol and marijuana. Responses to six questions were summed (a = 0.81).

Delinquent behavior
Adolescents reported the frequency with which they had damagedor destroyed property; hit or beat up another person; or taken something from a store without paying for it, over the past 12 months. Responses were summed (a = 0.84).

SEXUAL ACTIVITY

Adolescents in the ninth and 12th grades indicated: whether they ever had sexual intercourse, number of opposite gender partners over the past 12 months and frequency of birth control use. Responses were summed with higher scores indicating higher risk sexual activity (more partners and less use of birth control) (a = 0.98). Data on sexual behaviors were not collected on sixth graders.

SUICIDE ATTEMPTS

Adolescents completed two questions regarding suicidal ideation and behaviors, and indicated whether they had thought about, or attempted suicide, over a year ago, during the past year, both or never. Responses were summed with higher scores indicating increased suicidal risk (a = 0.54).
Strength of association between psychosocial variables and health- compromising behaviors were examined with Pearson's correlation coefficients separately among males and females.

Associations between psychosocial variables were also examined using Pearson's correlation coefficients. Multiple stepwise linear regressions were employed in analyzing associations between psychosocial variables and health-compromising behaviors.

Health-compromising behaviors were the dependent variables, and separate regressions were run on each behavior for the differentage and gender groups. The contribution of each psychosocial variable to the total explained variance in the behaviors and the totalpercent of variance explained by all of the psychosocial variables included in the analyses was determined.

LIFESTYLE, AND HEALTH

Few would deny that today's college students are under a lot of pressure. In addition to many usual stresses and strains incidentalto the college experience (e.g., exams, term papers, and the dreaded freshman 15), students today are faced with increasedcollege tuitions, burdensome debt, and difficulty finding employmentafter graduation. A significant population of non-traditional college students may face additional stressors, such as raising children or holding down a full-time job while working toward a degree.

Of course, life is filled with many additional challenges beyond thoseincurred in college or the workplace. We might have concerns with financial security, difficulties with friends or neighbors, family responsibilities, and we may not have enough time to do the things we want to do. Even minor hassles—losing things, traffic jams, and loss of internet service—all involve pressure and demands that can make life seem   like a struggle and that can compromise our sense of well-being. That is, all can be stressful in some way.

Scientific interest in stress, including how we adapt and cope, has been longstanding in psychology; indeed, after nearly a century of research on the topic, much has been learned and many insights have been developed. This chapter examines stress and highlights our current understanding of the phenomenon, including itspsychological and physiological natures, its causes an consequences, and the steps we can take to master stress rather than become its victim.

All lifestyle factors were associated with the mental   healthoutcomes. Better mental health was linked to higher frequency of physical and mental activity, moderate alcohol consumption (i.e. notincreased or no alcohol consumption), non-smoking, a body mass index within the range of normal to overweight (i.e. not underweight or obese) and a regular life rhythm. The more healthy lifestylechoices an individual makes, the higher life satisfaction and lower psychological distress he or she tends to have.

CHRONIC DISEASES [DIABETES, HYPERTENSION, CORONARY HEART DISEASE],

A chronic illness is "a long-lasting condition that can be controlled but not cured" (University of Michigan Center for Managing Chronic Disease, 2011). Examples in children include asthma, diabetes,cancer and organ failure. Most children and their families adapt well to living with a chronic illness. Some have greater difficulty with adjustment and coping, however. Adjustment problems can occur atthe time of diagnosis, or may arise later on, as the result of the chronic stress of living with an illness. Adjustment problems are alsomore likely in children who had prior behavioral or psychological problems, or in families with higher levels of conflict.

Children or families who are having difficulty coping with medical illness can be seen by Texas Children's experts in Psychology. Adjustment at diagnosis when a child is first diagnosed with a chronic illness, all families experience some combination of shock, disbelief, anger, fear and worry. Children may ask, "Why me?" And parents will ask, "Why did this happen to my child?" These are normal reactions to diagnosis and usually lessen with time. However, diagnosis of a chronic illness can be **traumatic** for some children and their parents. As many as 1 in 5 children and parents experience acute stress at the time of diagnosis that may benefit from additional support.

You may want to speak with a pediatric health psychologist oranother mental health professional if you or your child:
1. can't stop thinking about the diagnosis or worrying about the illness and its complications
2. can't sleep, can't concentrate, feel overly jittery or stressed
3. avoid any reminders of the illness
4. one or more of these symptoms lasts for more than 1-2 weeks

Many parents also **feel guilty** and worry that they did something to cause their child's illness. It is important to understand that there was nothing anyone did to cause the illness, and almost certainly nothing anyone could have done to prevent it.

CHRONIC ILLNESS AS CHRONIC STRESS

After diagnosis, families find that they have to make many changes to their daily routines to manage the illness effectively. Children maystart to think of themselves differently, and parents have to face a new set of worries. Living with a chronic illness can bring many challenges, including:
physical symptoms such as discomfort or pai
1.   treatments that can be unpleasant or difficult to followconsistently
2.   lifestyle changes, such as having to follow dietary restrictions
3.   the need for high levels of parental monitoring
4.   the need for more frequent medical attention, possiblyincluding repeated hospitalizations
5.   disruptions to normal life, such as missing school, or havingrestrictions on activities

6.	uncertainty regarding complications, long-term outcomes, or(in the case of an illness like cancer) possible recurrence

All of these factors can cause significant **chronic stress** for thechild, the parents, and other family members. Stress, in turn, can take a psychological toll on children and families. Psychological difficulties experienced by children with chronic illness include:
5. persistent worries and fears about the illness and its long-term effects
6. fear of dying
7. fear of the hospital or medical procedures
8. persistent sadness, anger, irritability, or excessive moodiness
9. changes in self esteem
10.	concerns about physical appearance and body image issues
11.	behavior problems social difficulties, especially getting tease

You may want to speak with a pediatric health psychologist oranother mental health professional if any of the problems above lastfor more than a week or 2, and either:
12.	cause your child distress
13.	disrupt sleep
14.	cause a loss of interest in fun things or activities
15.	create conflict with other people

PARENTING A CHILD WITH A CHRONIC ILLNESS

Parenting a child with a chronic illness can also be a source of significant stress for caregivers. It is important for parents to make sure to take care of themselves as well as their child, to manage daily stress, and to seek help from family, friends, community organizations, or mental health professionals when needed.

Chronic illness can also change how caregivers parent. Parents may become overprotective because of increased fears of their child's vulnerability. They may also become more reluctant to set limits for a child's behavior, especially if the child has experienced a life-threatening emergency or an extended period of hospitalization or treatment. In general, parents can help their child cope by:
16.	setting the same clear, consistent limits for behavior they would for any other child
17.	expressing warmth and support
18.	fostering as normal a life as possible

Developmental issue

Having a chronic illness can affect the normal course of a child's development in different ways. A chronic illness may limit the child from engaging in activities that contribute to development. For example, some children being treated for cancer may not able to attend school or see friends during treatment due to reduced immune system functioning; a child with a heart transplant may not be allowed to participate in sports; or a child with type 1 diabetes may not be allowed by parents to go on sleepovers at a friend's house due to concerns that the other parents will not know how to manage the illness. Sometimes these limits are set by the child's medical provider; at other times, limits are set by parents who may have become overprotective.

19.	It is very important to help a child with a chronic illness have asnormal a life as possible, within the bounds set by the medical team.
20.	Ask the medical team if you have any questions about whetheran activity is okay for your child.
21.	If you remain concerned about an approved activity, try to thinkthrough ways in which the possible risks can be minimized so that your child can participate safely.
22.	Seek out alternative activities that can provide similar experiences.

EFFECTS ON LEARNING

Some chronic conditions can be associated with learning problems. This can occur   because the child misses a lot of school due to health problems or for extended periods of medical treatment. Parents should speak to their child's school about developing a **504 Plan** for their child to ensure appropriate accommodations ar made so that their child can still access and receive a free and appropriate public education.

Some conditions and their treatment can also more directly result in learning or attention problems. Children with a chronic illness who are having difficulty with learning or attention can be seen by Texas Children's experts in Neuropsychology.

DEVELOPING AUTONOMY

For adolescents, chronic illness may disrupt changing relationships with parents and friends and interfere with the process of gaining independence and autonomy. An adolescent with a chronic illness may be less comfortable with becoming less dependent on parents. On the other hand, parents may become more resistant to theadolescent's efforts to act independently.

Some ways to address the conflict between normal development of independence, while still addressing health care needs of the chronic illness, include the following:
23. Involve adolescents in health-related discussions (for example,current concerns about their illness, treatment choices).
24. Teach adolescents self-care skills related to their illness.
25. Encourage adolescents to monitor and manage their owntreatment needs.
26. Encourage the development of coping skills to addressproblems or concerns that might arise related to their illness.
27. Encourage older adolescents to begin to meet with theirhealthcare providers themselves.

Continued parent involvement While it is important to encourage adolescents' increased autonomy, it is also important for parents to maintain continued involvement in illness management. Youth whose parents stay involved in chronic illness management in developmentally- appropriate ways tend to have much better control of their illnesses and their symptoms. The challenge is finding a good balance between parent involvement and youth independence, which parents can foster by:
28. Communicating openly. Allow the teen to openly express thoughts, feelings, preferences, problems and concerns related to illness management, and listen without judgment.
29. Working together to think through and solve problems related to illness management.
30. Not pushing independence before the adolescent is ready for it. Instead, ask what the adolescent wants to do more independently, and ask what you can do to help.

You might want to speak with a pediatric health psychologist if significant parent-child conflict arises around illness management.

RELATIONSHIPS WITH PEERS
Chronic illness and treatment may also interfere with time spent withpeers or in the school setting, which is the adolescent's primary social environment. Self-esteem issues related to acceptance of one's self and concerns about acceptance by others can be intensified by chronic illness and related treatment needs. To address these concerns, consider the following:

Encourage spending time with friends. Help problem-solve anypotential barriers
31. Discuss concerns about what information to share with friends.
32. Support children and adolescents who are bullied by peers.Enlist school personnel to address the bullying.
33. Encourage and assist friends in being supportive. Involvefriends' parents in this as needed.

ADHERENCE TO TREATMENT AND LIFESTYLE CHANGES
As adolescents with chronic illness learn more about their illnessand take more responsibility for its management, they will begin to make their own decisions about management. They may also experiment. For example, trials of decreasing their medication or nottaking it without consulting healthcare providers may occur. Teens may also make different decisions when they are alone versuswhen they are with friends; in general, they are less likely to complete illness management tasks when with friends. While these behaviors are developmentally normal, they create the need for continued parental monitoring and support.

34. Encouraging open discussions with teens around treatment choices, and taking a nonjudgmental approach to the choices they make, is crucial if parents want to continue to have an influence over these decisions.
35. Parents should view these attempts as opportunities for discussion and active problem-solving with their teen, rather than as deviations to be punished. If an adolescent does not complete a treatment task (like taking medication), encourage discussion of what happened and why and what can be done in the future, rather than reprimanding the teen
36. Teach and encourage use of problem-solving skills related to their illness. Ask questions, such as: "What do you think you would you do if...?"or "What do you think would happen if...?" Encourage adolescents to ask you the same kinds of questions.
37. Encourage teens to share their ideas and concerns with their healthcare providers.
38. Work on "team building" between the adolescent, parents, and healthcare providers.

BURNOUT
Angry or self-conscious feelings related to having a chronic illness can significantly affect adherence with recommended treatment or management techniques. Adherence may also decline over time due to disease management burnout, which is very common, especially among teens. Teens may come to feel discouraged, especially if it has proven difficult to gain good illness control, and this can progress to feelings of helplessness and hopelessness. To help:
39. Recognize how difficult and frustrating it can be to live with andmanage a chronic illness.
40. Ask if the youth feels burned out or discouraged about illness management.

41. Ask if the youth is getting the support he/she needs, and what parents and healthcare providers can do to help "lessen the load."

You might want to speak with a pediatric health psychologist if the youth
2 seems helpless or hopeless around illness management
3 is distressed about the illness or its management
4 seems sad more days than not
5 shows changes in sleep, appetite, interest, or grades
6 becomes withdrawn

TREATMENT AND CARE

Almost all families hit "bumps in the road" when living with a chronic illness. **Pediatric health psychologists** are experts in behavioral health, illness management, and adherence difficulties who useevidence-based treatment strategies to help children and their families cope with the difficulties of living with a chronic illness. Children, adolescents, and their families can be seen for a one-time consultation around illness management difficulties, brief behavioraltherapies, or longer-term individual or family outpatient therapy as needed.

DIABETES

Having diabetes can take its toll, with the different aspects of self- management often feeling overwhelming. The responsibility for managing diabetes lies almost entirely in the hands of the person with this life-long condition.

People with different types of diabetes often have distinctive psychosocial needs. This article focusses on type 2 diabetes which is the most common form of the condition

IMPACT ON QUALITY OF LIFE

The personal costs for those with type 2 diabetes are many. It can impact on relationships, on working and social life, and on psychological well-being, with a consequent effect on overall quality of life.

Constant monitoring, following a healthy diet and finding time for exercise can all lead to improved mental and emotional health.

People with diabetes are up to three times more likely to report symptoms of depression and these can be debilitating. For type 2 diabetes, £1.8 billion of additional costs to the NHS can   be attributed to poor mental health. However, less than 15% of people with diabetes have access to psychological support, in spite of the fact that psychological support improves health and cuts costs by 25%.

Poor mental and emotional well-being can lead to feeling less inclined to monitor blood glucose levels which then impact on self- management and diabetes control. People who feel   depressed often feel lethargic and so are less likely to exercise. Diet is   also very often affected with less healthy foods and more alcohol consumed. In addition, sleep is often affected (problems sleeping are one of the symptoms of depression), which can have a serious impact on overall quality of life.

SYMPTOMS OF DEPRESSION INCLUDE:

42. Feeling sad/depressed mood Lack of interest/enjoyment in daily activitie
43. Inability to sleep
44. Early waking
45. Tiredness/lack of energy
46. Loss of appetite
47. Feelings of guilt/worthlessness
48. Recurrent thoughts about death/suicide

EMOTIONAL DISTRESS

People with diabetes may also experience diabetes-related emotional distress and although there is a strong association between distress and depression, many people only report one or the other. Symptoms of diabetes-related distress include constantly worrying about blood glucose levels or the risk of getting diabetes complications, feeling angry about living with diabetes, and feeling guilty when going off track with managing diabetes self-care.

Distinguishing between symptoms of depression or diabetes-relateddistress through discussion with the diabetes nurse or GP, can help to decide what the most appropriate follow-up care should be offered.

For example a referral for counselling or other 'talking therapies', or diabetes education. The 'vicious cycle' (as described in **figure 1**) can be broken if appropriate support is given.

IMPORTANCE OF WELL-BEING

The importance of psychological and emotional well-being has now been recognised by not only Diabetes UK, but the National Institut for Health and Care Excellence (NICE) and there are guidelines for the management of diabetes and depression when they occur together.

NHS England has also recognised the importance of good mental health, advocating a holistic approach to care for people with diabetes which includes consideration of mental and emotional well-being as well as physical health (NHS England 2018). Diabetes UK has recommended that ever person with diabetes should be inreceipt of 15 healthcare essentials - including getting psychological and emotional support, and that receiving more integrated carewould improve outcomes and quality of life. This, they say, would also subsequently reduce healthcare costs.

A 'stepped care' approach to treating depression has been recommended by NICE which organises provision according to what is seen as the patient's specific needs.

IDENTIFYING THE SYMPTOMS

When someone goes to their GP to discuss feeling depressed or anxious, identification of symptoms starts with two questions:

- During the last month, have you often been bothered by feeling down, depressed or hopeless?
- During the last month, have you often been bothered by having little interest or pleasure in doing things?

If the answer is 'yes' to either of these questions, then further questions are asked in order to decide on the next step, and this is usually based on the severity of symptoms.

What support is available

A service available to all those identified as having depressive symptoms is the **Improving Access to Psychological Therapies** (IAPT) service. GPs usually make the referral, however self-referral is also an option. The IAPT service consists of talking therapies such as cognitive behavioural therapy.

NICE guidelines, based on existing evidence, also recommend the use of physical activity groups, motivational interviewing, and group or family therapy.

Some people prefer group rather than individual support as it can promote a sense of belonging, sharing stories and feeling lessisolated.

A recent systematic review of studies investigating the impact of different treatments in people with diabetes found that both psychological and pharmacological interventions had a moderate effect on depressive symptoms, but had no impact on quality of life. NICE are currently updating their guidance and evaluating the evidence which can inform their recommendations.

Specific guidelines for supporting people with long-term conditions (including diabetes) have only very recently (April 2018) been developed and are yet to be widely available. At the same time, direct access to psychological support in primary or secondary diabetes clinics remains scarce.

There is often a lack of confidence in talking about depression or other psychological and emotional problems, on the part of both the GP and the person with diabetes.

The treatment of diabetes and its physiological consequences is often seen as the main priority of care, with psychological well-bein further down the list, and worries about the most appropriate serviceto offer or receive are common.

DON'T BE AFRAID TO ASK FOR HELP

Asking for help with psychological problems can be difficult. Mental health problems still carry a stigma which can influence whether or not symptoms are expressed.

The language used within clinical settings can also influence the discussions. Using words such as 'adherence' or 'compliance' with treatment can have serious negative effects. Conversely, using non-discriminatory words can open up conversations and help identify the particular needs of the person with diabetes.

MORE SUPPORT IS NEEDED

In summary, diabetes can have a serious psychological and emotional impact, and can affect self-management as well as the individual's quality of life. A range of psychological problems can occur including depression, anxiety and diabetes-related distress.

Diabetes care service providers have acknowledged the extent of this problem and advocate a holistic approach to care which includes consideration of both physical and mental health.
It is recommended that psychological well-being is addressed in clinical consultations so that the most appropriate and person-centred care is provided, however there remains a shortage ofspecialist support.

Hypertension and Psychological Healt
High blood pressure (HBP) is also known as hypertension. It is becoming too common in the 21st century despite the fact people are more health conscious []. Research proves healthy diet and exercise are effective in lowering HBP []. However, the diagnosis of hypertension is not decreasing. The concept of a healthy life style must be holistic and consider all factors that contribute tohypertension. This requires identifying the connection of the systolic(top number) and diastolic (bottom number) pressure to the cause when developing a holistic treatment plan for each patient. Perhaps the 21st century treatment for hypertension patients includes total mind, body and soul.

KNOW YOUR NUMBERS

High blood pressure is a silent killer because it leads to heart attacks and strokes. Hospitals and doctor's office staff measure each patient's blood pressure to break the silent attack of HBP []. A patient hears their numbers and information about a healthy blood pressure reading during their visits to the doctor. A blood pressure (BP) reading has a top and bottom number referred as systolic and diastolic pressure []. In adults, a good systolic pressure is 120 mm Hg and a good diastolic pressure 80 mm Hg or less []. Each numberis a snap shot of each patient's healthcare needs.

Doctors rely on the BP measurement to guide them in developingan appropriate treatment plan for each patient. The systolic pressure is the measurement of the arteries contractions as the heart is compressing and a high number indicates stress on the arteries []. The diastolic pressure is the resting pressure the measurement of blood flow between each heartbeat and a high number indicates an elevation in pulse rate []. The differences between systolic and diastolic pressure is simply physical cause and mental causes. Therefore, a patient should know their numbers to make adequate lifestyle changes to have a good BP reading.

HEALTHY LIFE STYLE CHANGES

High blood pressure shakes the core of all patients and they want tocorrect the problem by any means necessary. Doctors prescribe medication, a healthy diet, and exercise to their patients and many follow the doctor's orders []. This treatment is effective in many patients. However, there are some patients living a healthy lifestyle and still have a high diastolic pressure []. The question they ask in frustration is what is causing a high diastolic pressure despite a healthy life style of diet and exercise. This leads to the analysis of stress and physical health [].

Psychological heath includes stress and anxieties. Therefore, it is necessary for a patient to seek the professional care of a psychiatrist to identify the stressors and develop a treatment plan []. There are also mechanics in psychiatric care because the endocrinesystem plays a vital role in releasing cortisol that affect the resting BP []. The 21st century is the era of holistic healthcare. Therefore, proper treatment for HBP should include psychiatric care. Medication is not the only treatment for HBP in regards to physical healthcare or psychological health care [].

A holistic care plan should use medications as the last option and if used it should be temporary as the patient makes their holistic care life style changes. A holistic plan of care for HBP is mind, body, and soul.

The mind, body, and soul treatment should align with the patient's beliefs. Many doctors and psychiatrist agree people become healthier when they reduce their exposure to a busy and nois environment]. Therefore, spending time in nature enjoying its serine sounds is therapeutic and reduces the cortisol levels causing elevations in diastolic pressure that will increase with time of systolicpressure []. A healthy life style goes beyond diet and exercise. The mind, body, and soul are a lifelong preventive care plan and an effective treatment plan for HBP.

CONCLUSION

Patients' lifestyles have an impact on their BP. Doctors need to assess holistically the cause of patient's HBP to provide an appropriate treatment plan. In   the 21st century, medication is not the first choice of treatment for HBP. Doctors encourage their patients to switch to a healthy diet, exercise, and relax []. However, relaxing is the most difficult part of the treatment plan for most patients who do not know the cause of their stress. In conclusion, physicians should recommend psychiatric care within their HBPtreatment plan.

PSYCHOLOGICAL TREATMENTS FOR CORONARY HEART DISEASE

Coronary heart disease is a common term for the buildup of plaque in the heart's arteries that could lead to heart attack. Butwhat about coronary artery disease? Is there a difference?

The short answer is often no — health professionals frequently use the terms interchangeably.

However, coronary heart disease , or CHD, is actually a result of coronary artery disease, or CAD, said Edward A. Fisher, M.D., Ph.D., M.P.H., an American Heart Association volunteer who is the Leon H. Charney Professor of Cardiovascular Medicine and also o the Marc and Ruti Bell Vascular Biology and Disease Program at the NYU School of Medicine.

With coronary artery disease, plaque first grows within the walls of the coronary arteries until the blood flow to the heart's muscle is limited. View an illustration of coronary arteries. This is also called ischemia. It may be chronic, narrowing of the coronary artery over time and limiting of the blood supply to part of the muscle. Or it can be acute, resulting from a sudden rupture of a plaque and formation of a thrombus or blood clot.

The traditional risk factors for coronary artery disease are high LDL cholesterol, low HDL cholesterol, high blood pressure, family history, diabetes, smoking, being post-menopausal for women and being older than 45 for men, according to Fisher. Obesity may also be a risk factor.

"Coronary artery disease begins in childhood, so that by the teenage years, there is evidence that plaques that will stay with us for life are formed in most people," said Fisher, who is former editor of the American Heart Association journal, ATVB. "Preventive measures instituted early are thought to have greater lifetime benefits. Healthy lifestyles will delay the progression of CAD, and there is hope that CAD can be regressed before it causes CHD."

Living a healthy lifestyle that incorporates good nutrition, weight management and getting plenty of physical activity can play a big role in avoiding CAD.

"Coronary artery disease is preventable," agreed Johnny Lee, M.D., president of New York Heart Associates, and an American Heart Association volunteer. "Typical warning signs are chest pain,shortness of breath, palpitations and even fatigue.

PSYCHONEUROIMMUNOLOGY [CANCER, HIV/AIDS]

In a nutshell, PNI studies the connection between psychological processes and the nervous and immune systems of the body. A more detailed description of PNI was given in an interview with Dr. Robert Ader, a Distinguished University Professor at the University of Rochester School of Medicine and Dentistry, and one of thepioneers of this rapidly growing branch of research. It reads as follows:

"Psychoneuroimmunology refers, most simply, to the study of the interactions among behavioral, neural and endocrine (or neuroendocrine), and immunologic processes of adaptation. Its central premise is that homeostasis is an integrated process involving interactions among behavior and the nervous, endocrine, and immune systems."

History

The field grew from the work of Russian psychologist IvanPavlov and his classical conditioning model. Pavlov was able tocondition dogs to salivate when they heard the ring of a bell by ringing a bell when they were given food. Eventually, they came to automatically associate the sound of the bell with the act of eating, so that when the food was no longer given, the sound of the bell would automatically cause them to salivate.

With PNI, Russian researchers conducted a series of experiments that showed that the body's other systems may be altered by conditioning as well. Although their research does not live up t today's rigorous standards, they were able to cause immunologic reactions in animals in much the same way that Pavlov created salivation in his dogs.

American researchers like Ader took the research further in the United States, and we now know for certain that immune responses can be enhanced or suppressed with a wide variety of conditioned cues. We also have a deeper understanding of the placebo effect— some researchers are beginning to believe that it might be a conditioned response as well.

PSYCHONEUROIMMUNOLOGY APPLICATIONS

Psychoneuroimmunology research sheds a great deal of light on many aspects of wellness and provides important research on stress. PNI studies have found may correlations between life eventsand health effects.

As PNI has gained greater acceptance in the scientific community, the finding that emotional states can affect immunity has been an important one, and research in this area helps us to gain a clearer understanding of stress and its effects on health. We are gaining a clearer understanding of the links between lifestyle and personality factors and immunity as research continues.

PSYCHONEUROIMMUNOLOGY: IMPLICATIONS FOR CANCER PROGRESSION AND TREATMENT

Research that has attempted to link psychosocial stressors with tumour development or progression has faced many obvious diYculties [1]. For example, stage of disease can have a profound eVect on how patients feel, and cancer treatments such as chemotherapy and radiation are associated with a number of side-eVects, including immunological alterations. One obvious area o interest is the possibility of inﬂuencing the course of cancer throughbehavioural interventions. Properly designed intervention studiesprovide a powerful tool for examining psychosocial factors. By random assignment of patients who have the same kind of stage of cancer to control and intervention conditions, researchers can assess psychological, immunological and disease changes. Following the initial demonstration of behaviourally mediatedimmune enhancement among older adults [21], a number of researchers have conﬁrmed our ﬁnding that stressreducing interventions can improve immune function [41].

One of the best studies in this area evaluated both the immediate and longer-term eVects of a 6-week structured group intervention that consisted of health education, enhancement of problem-solvingskills regarding diagnosis, stress management techniques such as relaxation, and psychological support [42, 43].

The patients had stage I or II malignant melanoma, and they had not received any treatment after surgical excision of the cancer. Noteworthy eVects included reduced psychological distress and signiﬁcant increases in the per cent of NK cells, as well as an increase in NK cell cytotoxicity, compared with controls.

A 6-year follow-up of these patients showed a trend towards greaterrecurrence, as well as a signiﬁcantly higher mortality rate in the control group than in intervention patients. The group diVerences remained signiﬁcant after adjusting for the size of the initial malignant melanoma lesion, a key risk factor.

Consistent with results of the intervention study with melanomapatients, Spiegel and colleagues [44] showed that a year of weekly supportive group therapy sessions with selfhypnosis for pain was associated with extended survival time in women with metastatic breast cancer. It is not known if these data reﬂect immunological alterations that inﬂuenced the course of the cancer, and a number of other interpretations are plausible. As the authors note, patients in the intervention condition could have been more compliant with medical treatment, and/or they might have had better health behaviours such as exercise and diet. Such behavioural differences could contribute to the observed outcome.

receiving chemotherapy for ovarian cancer. Comparisons of data obtained at home several days before a scheduled treatment showed greater lymphocyte proliferation when compared with samples drawn in the hospital just prior to the treatment, even after controlling for increased activity. Consistent with the interpretation ofthe process as conditioned immune suppression, patients also demons.

Other researchers have linked stress to poorer immune function in cancer patients whose immune systems are already aVected by disease. Among 116 women recently treated surgically for invasive breast cancer, greater stress (assessed via a self-reported measureof intrusive and avoidant thoughts and behaviours related to cancer)was associated with lower proliferative responses of PBLs to mitogens and to a monoclonal antibody against the T cell receptor [2]. Importantly, stress was also related to lower NK cell lysis, as well as diminished responsiveness of NK cells to rIFN-g.

Earlier studies from Levy and Herberman and colleagues [4, 5] had shown that three variables accounted for 51% of variance in baseline NK cell activity among women with breast cancer: patient `adjustment', lack of social support and fatigue/depressive symptoms. On reassessment of NK cell activity after 3 months, the investigators found that they could account for 30% of the varianc on the basis of baseline NK cell activity, fatigue/depression and lackof social support. Most importantly, NK cell activity remained markedly lower in patients with positive nodes than in patients with negative nodes, that is average levels ofNK cell activity were lower for patients with greater tumour burden. Even though neither radiation nor chemotherapy appeared to be related to subsequent NK cell activity, tumour burden was again associated with NK cell activity.

Additional data collected from breast cancer patients were consistent with evidence described earlier linking NK cell activitywith social support in healthy individuals [46]. Among women with stage I or II cancer, higher NK cell activity was associated with the perception of high-quality emotional support from a spouse or signiﬁcant other, perceived social support from the patient's physician, oestrogenreceptor negative tumour status, having an excisional biopsy as surgical treatment, and actively seeking social support as a major coping strategy.

PSYCHONEUROIMMUNOLOGY AND HIV DISEASE PROGRESSIONHIV / AIDS - A TABOO IN INDIAN SOCIETY

• million Indians are infected with the HIV virus; about 220,000 of them are children, with the tendency rising. The lack of education and the lack of condoms mean that the virus is spreading faster andfaster and more and more people are dying of AIDS - especially in the slums of the growing cities. More and more children are living there as so-called AIDS orphans , often being infected with the virusas well Among psychiatrists who treat patients with HIV/AIDS, the question of how psychosocial distress effects the progression of HIV disease is likely to arise. Even for healthy individuals, we are only beginning to clarify the complex pathways by which thoughts and emotions impact immune function. Due to the bidirectionality of the communications of the brain and the immune system, this is acomplicated scenario. The fact that HIV alters the function of the immune system during the course of its progression creates greater confounds to the understanding of these systems. We will address the rationale that progression from HIV infection to AIDS may be modulated by psychosocial factors, discuss possible reasons for conflicting findings and posit some clinically relevant recommendations drawn from research findings.

Among psychiatrists who treat patients with HIV/AIDS, the question of how psychosocial distress effects the progression of HIV disease is likely to arise. Even for healthy individuals, we are only beginning to clarify the complex pathways by which thoughts and emotions impact immune function. Due to the bidirectionality of the communications of the brain and the immune system, this is acomplicated scenario. The fact that HIV alters the function of the immune system during the course of its progression creates greater confounds to the understanding of these systems. We will address the rationale that progression from HIV infection to AIDS may be modulated by psychosocial factors, discuss possible reasons for conflicting findings and posit some clinically relevant recommendations drawn from research findings

PSYCHOSOCIAL VARIABLES: MODULATORS OF HIV DISEASE PROGRESSION?

The progression of HIV disease is highly variable   among individuals. Factors known to play a role in determining the rate of progression include the viral strain, genetic characteristics of the host immune system, co-infections with other pathogenic organisms(Zorilla et al., 1996) and health maintenance habits (e.g., diet, exercise, medical treatment). However, these factors do not fully explain the extreme degree of variability noted in the course of HIV disease (Cole and Kemeny, 1997).

Given that certain immune parameters are modulated   by physiologic mediators of the stress response (i.e., catecholamines and glucocorticoid hormones), it would seem logical to investigate the role of stress and other psychosocial factors in the progression of HIV infection. In fact, changes in immune function and disease susceptibility have been well documented in healthy individuals during times of psychic distress (Ader et al., 1995; Miller et al., 1997), and studies over the past 15 years have shown significant correlations between psychosocial variables and HIV progression. However, there have also been a number of studies showing no such correlation.

Stressful Life Experiences. Studies examining stressful life events and HIV have shown interesting but conflicting results. For example,Rabkin et al. (1991) studied 124 HIV-positive men and found no association between clinician-rated anxiety and CD4+ lymphocyte counts at study entry and at six-month follow-up. However, Evans etal. (1995), performing a similar cross-sectional study of HIV-positivemen, did show a significant correlation between   increased frequency of negative life events over the six months prior t interview and decreased CD8+ cytotoxic T-cells. Evans et al. (1997)continued with a two-year prospective study and found that not only were severe life stressors predictive of greater declines in some lymphocyte populations (natural killer [NK] cells and CD8+ cytotoxic lymphocytes), but also that such stressors increased the rate of HIVprogression to AIDS. The researchers emphasized that their results were noted only in those experiencing severe life stress, not stresses associated with everyday living. For every severe life stress reported, they found the risk of HIV disease progression to AIDS doubled. In their most recent work, these investigators followed 82 HIV-positive gay men at six-month intervals for up to 5.5years. They found that more cumulative life stress and less cumulative social support doubled or tripled the probability of progressing to AIDS (Leserman et al., 1999).

Depression. Studies examining the effect of depression on HIVprogression have had variable results. For example, Rabkin et al. (1991) found no correlation in their cross-sectional study between depression and CD4+ lymphocyte count or stage of HIV illness; however, a relationship was found between clinician-rated depression and increased report of HIV-related symptoms. In 1993, Burack et al. reported findings of a five-year prospective   cohortstudy that showed a significant correlation between depressive symptoms and more rapid decline in CD4+ lymphocyte counts,although not with increased HIV/AIDS-related morbidity or mortality.Conversely, in a similar eight-year study of 1,809 HIV-positive gay men, Lyketsos et al. (1993) found no significant   relationship between depression and indicators of HIV disease progression or clinical outcome. Likewise, results from a seven-year prospective cohort study of 402 gay men showed that depressed affect was associated with a greater AIDS-related mortality rate, although n correlation was found for measures of CD4+ lymphocytes (Mayne etal., 1996). In a meta-analytic review, Zorilla et al. (1996) concluded that no significant correlations could be made between depressive symptoms and markers of HIV disease progression. There did seemto be a relationship between depression and increased reporting of HIV-related symptoms.

Social Interaction. It is widely accepted that social isolation is a significant risk factor for several disease entities and that significant interruptions in social relationships can have deleterious effects. With regard to HIV/AIDS, this is exemplified among studies examining the death of an intimate partner, an event generallyassociated with bereavement and social role disruption.

Kemeny et al. (1995) studied 39 HIV-positive gay men who had experienced the death of an intimate partner within the previous 13 months. Looking at various markers of HIV progression pre- and postbereavement, they found significant increases in serum neopterin (a product of activated monocytes and a predictor of HIV disease progression) in the bereaved group. This finding was independent of ratings of depression, suggesting a qualitative difference between bereavement and depressive disorders. Anotherstudy unexpectedly found that greater self-reports of loneliness were associated with a slower decline in CD4+ lymphocytes over a three-year period, but not associated with time to AIDS diagnosis or AIDS-related death (Miller et al., 1997).

Similarly, in a study of socially and independently housed rhesus monkeys, Capatinio and Lerche (1998) found that greater social disruption around the time of inoculation with simian immunodeficiency virus correlated with a significantly increased rateof mortality. The rate of mortality also increased after inoculation I the animal was placed in a novel social environment versus individual housing. These findings, although yielding a variability of findings, suggest that social interactions may play an increasingly important role in understanding HIV disease progression.

Coping Responses. There is growing evidence that one's coping style may modulate the progression of HIV infection. For example, in a study by Byrnes et al. (1998), an increased measure of pessimism was related to lower NK-cell cytotoxicity in a group of HIV-seropositive black women at risk for cervical cancer. Furthering this hypothesis, Cole et al. (1996) found in a nine-year study thatthe degree of "closetedness," or concealment of gay identity, was strongly correlated with more rapid decline of CD4+ lymphocytes, more rapid progression to AIDS diagnosis and more rapid time to AIDS-related mortality. These findings were unrelated to health practices, medical treatment or other demographic differences and suggest a relationship between disease progression, poor coping and the stress of concealing one's sexual orientation.

Examining specific coping styles in a group of 74 gay men diagnosed with AIDS, Reed et al. (1994) showed that higher measures of "realistic acceptance" of their AIDS diagnosis was a significant predictor of decreased survival time. They point out that, in the past, researchers have shown unrealistic optimism to beassociated with better psychological adjustment and more active coping styles. Studies of the converse of this idea have found a "fighting spirit" to be associated with reduced progression to AIDS over a 12-month period (Solano et al., 1993). In an examination of the impact of perceived causes of events on HIV progression, Segerstrom et al. (1996) showed that the tendency to attributenegative events to the self was predictive of faster CD4+lymphocyte decline over the 18-month study period

FACTORS CONTRIBUTING TO THE DIFFERENCES OBSERVED IN STUDIES TO DATE
In attempting to compare the studies cited above, confounding elements include both the heterogeneity of the study populations and methodological differences among investigators. The majorityof studies have been conducted among groups consisting primarily of Caucasian, well-educated, homosexual men living in metropolitanlocations. However, even within this subgroup, there are variables that might skew study data (e.g., age group, unknown time since HIV infection, access to antiretroviral treatment and so forth).

A variety of methodological difficulties deserve mention. HIV/AIDS isan illness with an extraordinarily long latency period, so following patients even for several years may yield no substantive change in disease status. Putative immunologic changes brought about bypsychosocial factors tend to be small, necessitating larger samples to reveal significant findings (Cole et al., 1997). Many psychiatric disorders tend to be recurring, time-limited entities, and our measurement techniques for these typically yield only a cross- sectional glimpse of mental health at a given time. These factors could preclude significant findings in a disease like HIV/AIDS, whichhas a lengthy asymptomatic phase (Zorilla et al., 1996).

Currently, several known laboratory findings correlate with HIV progression, but their predictive value is questionable. The most common marker, the CD4+ lymphocyte, is predictive of increased risk for opportunistic infections once it drops below a critical level. Another promising marker is the plasma viral load. However, withthe advent of newer antiretroviral therapies, CD4+ lymphocyte levels can rise markedly and viral load can become undetectable foryears

CLINICAL RECOMMENDATIONS AND APPLICATIONS: LENGTHIER STUDIESARE NEEDED
Many studies give us hope that psychosocial interventions can not only improve our patients' quality of life, but also improve theirphysical health. For example, a study of 10 HIV-positive men by Taylor (1995), showed that behavioral stress management over a 20-week period significantly slowed the rate of CD4+ lymphocyte decline. These results are tempered by conflicting findings such as those of Mulder et al. (1995). Working with 26 asymptomatic, HIV- positive men in either cognitive-behavioral group therapy orexperiential group therapy, these researchers found no significant differences in CD4+ lymphocyte changes between group members and controls over a 24-month period. Lengthier studies of larger populations are clearly needed to elucidate further findings and to translate them from laboratory data into real-world scenarios.

Exercise training has been studied among several HIV-positive cohorts, revealing numerous psychological benefits including decreases in anxiety and depression and increases in active, positive coping styles. In a review of pertinent literature, LaPerriere et al. (1997) concluded that a typical regimen of aerobic exercise can result in increases in CD4+ lymphocyte counts in all HIV- positive patients, except those with AIDS. However, even among AIDS patients, the CD4+ lymphocyte counts remained stable overan 18-month study (whereas control patients' levels continued to decline).

The impact of HIV on neural tissue remains questionable. There is evidence, at least in the case of depression, that HIV-positive individuals respond to antidepressant therapy at rates similar toseronegative controls. The side-effect profiles of these medication also seem to differ minimally based on HIV status (Rabkin et al., 1994).

A significant finding about HIV and depression in the meta-analysis by Zorilla and colleagues (1996) was that depression was associated with increased reporting of HIV physical symptoms, regardless of objective markers of physical disease. Depressed HIV-positive individuals may have a more painful experience of HIV illness, regardless of objective physical signs and markers. Also, alleviating depression in some cases may facilitate compliance with medication regimens and medical follow-up, improve self-care, and decrease self-destructive behavior-all variables associated with diminished morbidity and mortality (Stober et al., 1997).

Overall, evidence remains inconclusive regarding the role of psychosocial factors in HIV disease progression, as well as the long-term effectiveness of interventions directed at such factors. However, it is certain that psychiatric disorders and social stressors occur frequently during the course of HIV disease. While it is unclear whether specific psychiatric and psychosocial interventions will extend life or improve physical health among HIV/AIDS patients,we do know definitively that treatment can alleviate psychiatric disorders, relieve distress, and improve quality of life and suchcritical variables as treatment adherence.

With more HIV-positive individuals being seen in general psychiatricpractice, one should not underestimate the positive effects of comprehensive psychiatric care

WHAT IS PSYCHOLOGY AND TECHNOLOGY INTERFACE: DIGITAL LEARNING; DIGITAL ETIQUETTE: CYBER BULLYING; CYBER PORNOGRAPHY: CONSUMPTION, IMPLICATIONS; PARENTAL MEDIATION OF DIGITAL USAGE?

PSYCHOLOGY AND TECHNOLOGY INTERFACE:

Human-computer interaction (HCI) is the study of how people interact with computing technology. One major area of work in the field focuses on the design of computer systems. The goal is to produce software and hardware that is useful, usable, and aesthetically pleasing.

A closely aligned area is the evaluation of systems in use. This is of course related to design, because to know if a design is useful or usable requires observing it in use. However, this also extends tothe study of the larger social consequences of use. Increasingly, evaluation takes place at multiple levels of analysis: the individual, the group, the organization, and the industry or societal sector.

The methodological and conceptual issues at these different levels of evaluation are quite different. Psychologists are typically most interested in the smaller levels of aggregation, though Landauer (1995) attempted to provide a largely psychological account of the "productivity paradox," a phenomenon first identified by economists who found a disappointing lack of correlation between the amount ofmoney invested in information technology and changes in industry productivity measures

This chapter updates and expands the last review of HCI in the Annual Review of Psychology (Carroll 1997). There has been steady growth in the field since then, and in our brief chapter we canonly highlight some of the most significant changes. We also give explicit attention to the emergence of research at the group and organizational level, often referred to as computer-supportedcooperative work or CSCW.

The field of HCI is fundamentally interdisciplinary. The fields ofcognitive, social, and organizational psychology are all important to research in the area, but other social sciences such as sociology and anthropology have played key roles, as have such related fieldsas communication, management, operations research, and ergonomics.

Also, a variety of technical specialties from computer science are important. Research in HCI requires literacy in the related fields andoften involves multidisciplinary collaboration. Some think of HCI asa purely applied field.

However, being applied does not mean lacking in relevance to basicscience. Stokes (1997) argued that the quest for fundamental understanding and considerations of use are two separate dimensions of a 2 × 2 table rather than opposite ends of a continuum. He used Pasteur as an example of research that sought both fundamental understanding and practical solutions.

Whereas some research in HCI is close to purely applied, as we hope toshow in this review, much of it falls in Pasteur's quadrant.

THE SCIENCE OF HUMAN COMPUTER INTERACTION

Theoretical advances in HCI are proceeding on a number of different fronts. Modeling of the integration of perceptual-cognitive motor processes to illuminate the moment-by-moment behavior people exhibit with computers has become more detailed. At the more social level, there is work on distributed cognition, focusing on the interplay of people with their teammates and the artifacts of theirinteraction.

Another class of tasks, that of information retrieval, is receiving attention from HCI researchers. What we do not have yet is a detailed model of social interaction or of some of the larger issues ofadoption of innovation. There is significant work to be done tounderstand what might be unique about the adoption of computationas an innovation, because computational artifacts can be designed in so many different ways.

Human Computer Interaction Work on Information Retrieval Whereas most of the theory and applications in HCI of the 1980s and early 1990s focused on computationally supported office applications such as word processors and spreadsheets, one of the major theoretical advances of the late 1990s came in   an examination of information-retrieval behavior. Spurred by the adventof the World Wide Web and ubiquitous "surfing" behavior, Pirolli & Card (1999) investigated how people decide to continue in a line of searches and when to jump to a different source or search string.

To model this behavior they drew on foraging theory from biology. They saw the analogy between the movement of animals from one food source to another (a "patch") and people's movement from oneinformation source to another.

They modeled the moment-by-moment decisions people make in their assessment of the value of what they see in search results to predict when they would pop back up to a high level change in a search string or a completely different source such as stopping searching the web and asking a reference librarian. This work also highlighted the importance of the display of the search results in the way it gives clues ("scents") as to whether further selection of an item is likely to be valuable ("to bear fruit"). So, for example, if a Google search returns only headers or urls, it has a less informative"scent" than a display of the sentence fragments that surround the words that match the search string.

These bits of information give the user clues as to whether the selection of that item is likely to be useful. The Card and Pirolli information-foraging work is remarkable not only in its   novelty oftask and approach, but in the variety of methods they bring to play in their work. They motivate the investigation with some descriptionsof real people searching for information—a team of MBAs doing an industry analysis and a consultant writing his monthly report on a topic. From phenomena gleaned from these cases, they worked with mathematical foraging theory, applying various concepts and equations to information rather than food-seekingbehavior. Of particular relevance here were calculations on the time a person would spend in a fruitful region of information beforemoving on to another and the factors that drove the decision to move. They then moved to modeling the moment-bymoment behavior of people conducting their search with an ACT-IF model (the ACT-R model applied to information foraging, IF).

The mathematical analyses show aggregate behavioral trends (e.g.,average time to linger as a function of richness of the scent), whereas the ACT-IF model allowed them to explore various mechanisms that might account for this behavior. They concluded with an empirical laboratory study of people making such switching decisions in a particular information-retrieval system called th "Scatter/Gather" interface. They made very specific predictions of when someone would stop searching a source (when the average value of a found item dropped below an estimated middle point). They also encouraged designs to give "scent," hints as to the ultimate value of continuing searching on a particular path, such as meaningful labels and revealing search results.

USER INTERFACE DEVELOPMENTS

As computing technology changes, new user interface challenges arise. For instance, in the early days of personal computing screen displays were mostly command lines in green or yellow on a black background. Editing a manuscript included placing explicit formatting characters in the text. With the emergence of graphical user interfaces (GUIs), whole new classes of issues emerged, as well as new opportunities for tapping into key cognitive and perceptual processes. Much of the design of early GUIs was influenced by psychological research (e.g., Johnson et al. 1989). Such systems have been around long enough that they have achieved some level of stability in design, even across different hardware and software platforms.

Now all kinds of new situations are emerging that are challenges to humancomputer interaction specialists. We briefly describe some examples of these and indicate the character of some of the psychological issues involved. As applications move from the desktop to more mobile, immersive environments and to a wider setof users, there remain a number of challenges for basic psychology.How do people understand aspects of the digital world as it isembodied in these various devices? How do we capitalize on the strengths of each human, coupling them with assistance from computing, to bring about the most in a productive, satisfying life Mobile Devices In the past decade a wide variety of small mobile devices have appeared. The most common are what are called personal digital assistants or PDAs. These are small handheld devices that have increasingly sophisticated computationalcapabilities.

The user interface challenges are daunting. These devices typically have small screens, and interactions are with a stylus and a small set of buttons. Some models have optional folding keyboards that allow for more traditional interactions. Despite these user interface challenges, such devices have a number of very useful functions and are very popular. Combinations of mobile devices, such as the merging of PDAs and cell phones, are just appearing. One specialized user interface issue is how to integrate such mobile devices with more traditional computing. For instance, Milewski & Smith (2000) developed a digital address book with location sensors that could be accessed from a regular workstation or from a PDA and that provided information about the availability ofothers that could be used to coordinate phone calls regardless of where the participants might be. The interface had to be adapted to the capabilities of each device in a way that   users found intuitiveand natural.

DIGITAL TECHNOLOGY ON LEARNING

Over our first few blogs, let's take a look at the effects of digitaltechnology on learning. We'll begin in the classroom.

Does technology interfere with classroom learning?Yes
According to one teacher survey regarding the problem with technology in schools (Washington Post 2013):
Nearly 90% of teachers felt technology has created   a distracted generation with short attention spans.
60% felt it hindered writing and face-to-face communication; i.e., communication with full sentences and longer has lost out to short snippets in writing or media.
Almost 50% felt it hurt critical thinking and homework ability.
76% felt students were conditioned to find quick answers.
In short, technology is changing the way our students learn, and notalways for the better.
In another survey, university students were asked how often they use their cell phones while in class for non-class related uses (Baron 2015). The average college student reported such use 11 times daily. 15% of students used their cell more than thirty times during class. All of this activity comes at a price in learning. In one study, students who sent text messages while watching a lecture had exam scores 19% below those who did not text (Thompson 2014).
When students were asked themselves about texting during class time, the following percent of them agreed or strongly agreed:
77% felt that receiving text messages hurts my ability to learn during lecture. 72 % felt that sending text messages hurts my ability to learn during lecture 37% felt that they get distracted when someone else receivesa text during class.
31% felt that they get distracted when someone else sends atext during class.

Thus, students recognize that texting in school not only interferes with their own learning, but also interferes with other student's attention—yet 49% of them still felt it was okay to text during class (Rosen, 2012).

Not surprisingly, allowing web access   (i.e., not just texting access) to students during a lecture doesn't fare well, either. One group of students was allowed to surf the web during class, and the other kept their laptop closed. Students did indeed look at lecture related sites, but also went shopping, watched videos and caught up on e- mail. Even those students who surfed only on topics related to the lecture showed significantly worse memory of the lecture's content than those who kept their laptop closed (Carr 2011).

Yet, multiple studies reveal that the majority of students say thatthey use their electronic devices during class to text, browse, or consume media. The results of these studies agree with my own informal survey of my patients who, when asked, almost uniformly say that students are using the classroom laptops/iPads for non- educational activities. Even those who have monitored or limited Internet access still use their laptops for offline gaming. If an adult comes around, they simply hit a button which switches the screen toa legitimate activity. The CD (remember those?) version of MAD magazine even contains a "panic button" which, if pressed when an adult checks in, pulls up a Word document that reads something t the effect that, "I can't believe my parents fell for this again." School systems that are switching to all digital experiences for   their students must ask themselves if the advantages are worth the distractions.

Digital etiquette, or netiquette as it is sometimes referred to, is a basic set of rules pertaining to behaviour that needs to be followedto ensure the Internet is better for all users. Basically it means "the use of good manners in online communication such as e-mail, forums, blogs, and social networking sites Digital etiquette, or netiquette as it is sometimes referred to, is a basic set of rules pertaining to behaviour that needs to be followedto ensure the Internet is better for all users. Basically it means "the use of good manners in online communication such as e-mail, forums, blogs, and social networking sites" (Digital Citizenship, Auburn University. n.d.).

Etiquette, the word, means "The forms required by good breeding orprescribed by authority in social or official life". The origins of the word stems from the French word "ticket"; if you knew the etiquette for the group or society you would have a 'ticket' to gain access (Shea, V. 2004).

Importance of Netiquette
So why is netiquette so important? When we communicate face- to-face, it is important to note that 55% of the communication is made up of body language, 38% is the tone of voice, with the remaining 7% being the actual words (Psychology Today (Thompson, J. 2011). When communicating on a phone we lose the body languagecomponent but the tone is still there to support the message.

However, communicating online, or in the written form, we lost 93%of the communication – the words become the sole mechanism for communication! As a result misunderstandings occur without thes non-verbal cues.

So how do we provide these non-verbal cues in digital communication? Informally we use emoticons to aid the message,but formally this is a lot harder. Most formal communication occurswithin a business context, so netiquette becomes vital in our communication as businesses rely heavily on building and maintaining relationships.
Netiquette is even more important when we consider the longevityand the reach of the communication. The lack of netiquette can cause substantial problems in the workplace and schooling.

Although there has been a reduction in poor netiquette, it is still anissue that has ramifications beyond socially acceptable norms Etiquette and Business. Business is about building relationships, which at times can take years. Creating the rapport is incredibly important in establishing trust, authenticity and credibility. Any disregard for netiquette can break this down with a single email, post or online comment. It is key for businesses to focus on the digital skills of their employees;moreover the focus should be on communication with a nuance ondigital communication.

Etiquette and Society
We know that the socio-cultural environment has the deepest, strongest, and perhaps most prevailing effect on social behaviour.In fact etiquette are societal norms, therefore netiquette would be the rules society dictates we utilise when we are online.

The Online Disinhibition Effect
People disclose or act out more frequently, at times more intensely, when they are online. More so than when they are off- line. Becauseof this loss of inhibition, users show tendencies, such as being moreaffectionate, more open, and less guarded, in an attempt to achieve emotional well being (Suler, 2004 Role of Rules and Policy We communicate daily, be it in a social, business or academic context, and the way in which we engage will differ. Without any form of 'guidelines' or rather rules and policy on conduct, our interactions will degenerate and result in negative consequences.(N)Etiquette is all about the code of behaviour established for communicating and behaving

Electronic Standards of Conduct
Electronic Standards of Conduct is a set of standards on social, environmental and ethical issues within the context it is provided. Most companies have such standards, often referred to as Acceptable Use Policy (AUP). This is often used as a guideline for employees and users, but also in terms of managing staff. Given that employees represent the company, even outside of their normalworking hours, therefore some standards need to be in place.

Employees in breach of these standards may find themselveswithout a job, as it is seen as part of their contract with the company.

Virginia Shea's Netiquette Guidelines
These guidelines will differ, in terms of the context and the medium available. However, there are some core principles that we need to be aware of and adhere to. According to Shea (1994), an academicwho has been dubbed the 'network manners guru', these guidelinesare:
1. Remember the Human Never forget that the person reading yourcommunication is actually a person with feelings and can get hurt. Essentially never say anything online that wouldn't say to your reader's face. Adhere to the same standards of behaviour online that you followin real life Be ethical in your engagement and know that breaking the law is bad netiquette Know where you are in cyberspace The netiquette required will differ from domain to domain. If you are in a forum of experts, your netiquette should reflect respect. Whereas if you are in a chat roomwith a group of friends (you know in real life) then the netiquette willdiffer!
2. Respect other people's time and bandwidth When sharing files ordocuments, bear in mind the audience's bandwidth.

Furthermore, make sure you read the FAQs first before asking mundane questions where the answers already exist. If you disagree with a group's discussion, don't waste their (or your) time by telling them how stupid they are: Just stay away.

3. Make yourself look good online Check grammar and spelling before you post. Most people judge others' intelligence based onthe use of grammar and spelling. Only post on things you know about, it is not worth it to look like the fool.
4. Share expert knowledge Offer answers and help others whereyou can Help keep flame wars under control Don't respond to flame-bait,don't post spelling or grammar flames, and apologise if you have done so or perpetuated a flame-war.
5. Respect other people's privacy Don't give out other people's details, online or offline.
6. Don't abuse your power The more power you have, the moreimportant it is how you use it.
7. Be forgiving of other people's mistakes We all were once a newb (and no we don't mean noob – those who know little and haveno will to learn any more).

Bad Etiquette Examples

— Although these are not the only examples of bad netiquette theseexamples may give an idea of the things that are taboo: Don't type in CAPS – it is considered shoutin

— Don't spam

— Don't use offensive language

— Don't steal other people's identity

— Don't distribute illegal material

— Don't flood

— Don't expect a response straight away

— Don't broadcast only; engage with others Don't 'reply-all' for a personal conversation Don't ask a question that can be found on the site or on Google"(Melin, 2013).

CYBERBULLYING FROM A PSYCHOLOGICAL PERSPECTIVE

The stereotype bully used to be the big kid in the school taking smaller children's dinner money or the colossal 'Miss Trunchball' terrorizing the tiny kids in Roald Dahl's book, 'Matilda'. In recent years the definition of bullying has extended beyond the school playground and we are more likely to recognize that the capacity tobully others is not limited to those with large bodies.

Over the past twenty years, as the internet and mobile phones havebecome embedded in our lives, we have heard about children and adults who have been targeted by bullies online. We seem to have improved our understanding of how bullies operate and we are more likely to believe the stories of those who have been bullied butwe do not seem to have made much progress in preventing bullyingor dealing with bullies.

For those of us who are less familiar with social media or do not feelconfident in understanding the online context it might feel overwhelming and confusing if, either professionally or personally someone seeks our support or advice on addressing cyberbullying. Ihope that the following information serves as a way of familiarizing oneself with some of the issues that might come up and suggest ways we can support people who have experienced cyberbullying.

What is cyberbullying?
'Cyberbullying' is a range of behaviours that people use to intimidate, shame or alienate another person online. Cyberbullying includes, but is not limited to, using offensive or dehumanizing language against someone; blackmail; 'outing' someone; threatening physical violence. In the same way that bullies often tryto isolate someone 'in real life' they might also try to rally others to isolate someone else in the online context and/or in 'real life'.

What distinguishes cyberbullying from face to face bullying?
In the past few years there have been several cases of high profilepeople being bullied online. Most notably, Twitter, has enabled people to communicate with famous people in a way that wasn't previously possible and there are many people who have used thisopportunity to express their racist, misogynistic and homophobic beliefs directly at their target.

One of the most striking aspects of these cases is the way that a'pack' descends onto the scene and, also, how online platforms appear to be ill-equipped to deal with bullying and so people aresometimes 'bullied off' the platform.

The internet also enables a person to bully strangers, without geographical limitations, via social media, comment sections, datingapps etc. in a way that wouldn't have been possible previously Additionally, a cyberbully can send abusive messages at any moment, not limited by the time restrictions of face to face contact.

Young people who have experienced cyberbullying describe a feeling of not being able to get away from it; that there is no respite.Older people might think that the solution is to disconnect from the online spaces where the bully can send messages or, perhaps, even to disconnect from social media altogether but it seems that young people are usually unwilling to sacrifice the more positive interactions they have in those online contexts in order to avoid thebully. Young people's online lives are often so embedded in their day to day lives telling them to quit social media is like telling them to stop going to the town centre so they can avoid the bully.

WHERE DOES CYBERBULLYING HAPPEN?

The most popular online social media platforms are facebook, instagram, twitter, snapchat and tumblr and the most popular mobilephone applications for sending messages and photos are WhatsApp and SnapChat.

However, there are always new platforms coming and going and it'sdifficult to keep up with the trends in the lesser known platforms andto understand what they entail. The NSPCC website 'net aware' (link in references section below) is very helpful as it provides descriptions of different apps and social media platforms and gives advice on how to use them as safely as is possible.

When we're thinking about how to help or protect others from cyberbullying it's important to be aware that platforms such as Netflix (TV and film streaming service), videogames and music apps(e.g Spotify) that are not necessarily marketed as 'social media' or communication apps also provide the possibility to send message (and therefore provide another platform for bullies to send abusivemessages).

AT WHAT AGE DOES CYBERBULLYING BEGIN?

Most of us will have observed, experienced or participated in bullying at primary school, so we know that primary school aged children do have the capacity to bully others face to face. It would therefore follow that primary school aged children who are using social media are not immune from bullying others or being bullied byothers online.

Since the emergence of smart phones around 2010 it seems that more and more parents use mobile phones and/or portable devices to entertain or occupy babies and small children. Following on from this, it seems plausible that a child's first negative online experiencemust be becoming progressively younger and that it's not unrealisticthat their first experience of cyber bullying (whether it is observing, participating or being on the receiving end) could happen whilst theyare still attending primary school.

THE PROFILE OF THE CYBERBULLY

Most adults would admit to having engaged in some form of bullying, no matter how briefly, at some point in our lives. And, likein most other areas of human behaviour, it seems unlikely that a person who engages in protracted bullying is categorically differentfrom the rest of us but, rather, is more likely to be at the more severe end of personality traits that we all have: jealousy, obsessionality and lacking empathy (callousness).

As is the same with the face to face context, cyber bullying can provide a way for individuals to project their own feelings of distressinto another person. It also seems plausible that a nasty messag provides the sender with some temporary excitement or temporarilyrelieves some feelings of frustration. By sending nasty messages under the cloak of the internet (not necessarily anonymously) the sender is protected from any possible physical backlash from the receiver. However, they have also left an 'electronic trail' that could land them in trouble with their employer, their school, the online platform, or the police. Perhaps this is one of the reasons for the 'pack' behaviour mentioned previously: that bullies have a feeling of'safety in numbers' and if the pack unleash their anger and frustration on particular individuals they feel that they are less likely to be sanctioned than if they are the sole bully.

A long standing explanation of the behaviour of bullies in face to face contexts is that they are people who are unable to form a positive connection with others and so a negative, destructive communication is more rewarding for them than to be alone or isolated. It seems plausible that this explanation also holds up forcyberbullies.

DRAWING ON PROFESSOR PAUL GILBERT'S THEORIES TO UNDERSTANDCYBERBULLYING

Professor Gilbert's psychological theories have long since drawn onbroader social and evolutionary theories to make sense of individualfeelings and behaviours. It is useful to be reminded that, as human beings, we are inherently social creatures. It is also helpful to hold inmind that the vast part of our physical and mental evolution occurred during the hundreds of thousands of years prior to the first civilisations; the internet era of the last twenty years is less than a blink of an eye in the big picture of human evolution. Which leaves the question of how well our minds are equipped and/or able t adapt to the rapid technological changes that are happening in ourlives.

Gilbert (2006) outlines our most basic behaviour displays and defences: courting, sharing, fight, flight, submission and freezing and our basic cognitive competencies: Theory of Mind; symbolic representations of ourselves and others; and meta cognitions and meta presentations. Perhaps one of the reasons why smart phoneshave become so pervasive is because they draw on so many of ourmost primitive cognitive and physical capacities.

It seems that many people are emotionally attached to their mobilephones in a more profound way than other electronic devices. Thisemotionally attachment makes sense if the phone is recognised asa device that enables us to meet some of our most primitive needs.

Negotiating our social ranking is the one of the primitive activities that we use mobile phones for. I remember in 1997 when I was a waitress in Pizza Hut in Manchester and customers first began to put their mobile phones on the tables; when just having a mobile phone was a way to increase social ranking. Now, mobile phones are ubiquitous but provide a way of accessing higher social rank through the popularity or cleverness of the images or information that we share. And for those who have gained social rank via socialmedia, or aspire to gain social rank via social media, it is not surprising that they will try to resist losing that rank if the bullies come along.

It's also helpful to be reminded of Gilbert and McGuire's (1998) workon aggressive and attractive strategies for gaining social rank as, again, the very primitive nature of these behaviours fits well in the context of understanding online behaviour. I think this work helps to explain the polarisation that appears to be endemic to Twitter I particular. Gilbert and McGuire outline how, to gain and maintain social rank, people use either 'attractive' strategies such as showingtalent and competence in order to be valued and stimulate positive affect in others or they use 'aggressive' strategies such as authoritarianism, coercion or threats in order to make others fearful,inhibited or submissive.

So far, we have outlined several motivations for why people bully others online: feeling emboldened to express their offensive beliefs because others are doing so; projection of their own unwanted, unpleasant feelings into another person; personality traits on the severe end of the dimensions of jealousy, obsessionality and/or lackof empathy (callousness); attempts to use aggressive tactics to increase their social rank and/or inhibit someone else's social rank.

Supporting those who have been shamed online by Bullies attempt to shame others in a range of ways; from mocking them to sharing their videos or photos, particularly those of a sensitive nature. In face to face contexts this is bad enough but the permanence and the possibility of wide distribution online make things even worse.

One way of partly relieving shameful feelings is when we meet others who are willing or able to empathise with us. At the end of the Netflix documentary 'Audrie and Daisy' (2016) Daisy meets other teenage girls who were also bullied (online and face to face)by their peers after reporting sexual assaults to the police and themeeting appears to go some way towards relieving feelings of shame for those concerned Professor Gilbert's book, 'The Compassionate Mind' (2009) is a useful resource for developing self-compassion as an antidote tofeelings of shame.

Where bullies have distributed videos or images that are of a sexualnature and there is recourse to legal avenues it seems plausible that obtaining justice through the legal system might help to relieve some of the feelings of shame.

Supporting those who have been frightened by bullies online When bullies are making threats or have made threats the first stepshould always be to ensure the person's safety by contacting the police.

Paladin is a UK service offering advice and support to people who are being stalked and also provides advice to professionals who areworking with people who are being stalked.

It is also important to contact the support services for the online platforms where the bullying has taken place to ensure that the intimidation is prevented from reoccurring. Each social media platform has its own code of conduct and sanctions if the rules arebroken.

In terms of providing emotional support to those who have felt frightened by online bullies the most important priority is to ensurethat the person is now safe. If we can be sure the person is now physically safe only then can we support them in processing their feelings of anxiety about what happened in the past.

It is important to take people's emotional reactions to cyber bullyingas seriously as we would if the bullying was face to face It might be that the person continues to feel anxious because they are focused on thoughts of 'what could've happened', 'what could'vegone wrong'. In these cases we should validate the persons worriesbut help them trace the actual chain of events and to focus on the actual outcomes rather than the 'what could have beens'.

THE CONSEQUENCES OF HAVING BEEN BULLIED

I have worked with people in their eighties who continue to experience distressing memories of being bullied in school; for others, maybe the horrible memories do diminish but in every case we should always take the person's experience of being bullied seriously and listen carefully to the details of the particular situation so that we can offer the best and most appropriate support possible.

I have worked with families who have taken their child out of schooldue to bullying only for it to happen in the new school. In these cases it must be very difficult for the child not to believe that the problem is with them when, in reality, starting a new school is likelyto be a moment of vulnerability that bullies are vigilant to. It seems important to ensure that if the decision to change schools is made that the child receives proper support on how to approach starting their new school in light of their previous experiences.

From working across the lifespan we know that people who have experienced face to face bullying continue to experience the consequences for many years after: finding it difficult to trust others,internalising the bully's voice and so on. As online bullying is a relatively new phenomenon only time will tell if the consequences are as longstanding. What we do know is that people who have been bullied in either of these contexts have taken their own lives indicating that the short term impact of cyber bullying can be as devastating as face to face bullying

CONCLUSION

I've met several young people who have been worried that if they tell someone about the bullying that they're experiencing that 'it willmake things worse'. Of course, this plays directly into the hands of the bully who seeks to isolate the person that they're bullying. By listening very carefully, paying attention to the fine details of the situation and providing emotional support to the young person we can work out the most appropriate solutions together.

Schools, social media platforms, families and any other place wherepeople are interacting are vulnerable to the possibility of bullying taking place. In terms of supporting people (of all ages) who are targeted by cyber bullies, I think we should have at least a basic understanding of social media in order to provide appropriate support and advice. As in any other form of tyranny the minority of people who engage in cyber bullying depend on the fragmentation, impassivity and indifference of the wider society. By having a better understanding of social media, even if we do not have a personal interest in it ourselves, we will be better able to provide appropriate support and advice to those who are targeted by cyber bullies.

PORNOGRAPHY

A study of Internet pornography users suggests a person's own feeling of being addicted to online pornography drives mental healthdistress, not the pornography itself.

Researcher Joshua Grubbs, a doctoral candidate at Case Western Reserve University's Department of Psychological Sciences, said the finding adds a fresh perspective to commonly held concerns thatInternet pornography can be a threat to mental health. Th research, funded by the John Templeton Foundation, suggests thatfeeling addicted to Internet pornography is associated with depression, anger, and anxiety, but that actual use of pornography is not.

Grubbs is part of a research team that did a study titled "PerceivedAddiction to Internet Pornography and Psychological Distress: Examining Relationships Concurrently and Over Time." The articleis now published in Psychology of Addictive Behaviors, a journal ofthe American Psychological Association.

With Grubbs on the research team are Nicholas Stauner and Julie J. Exline, also of Case Western Reserve University; Kenneth I. Pargament of Bowling Green State University, and Matthew J.Lindberg of Youngstown State University.

Grubbs said Internet pornography viewing online is increasingly common, more among adult males than adult females. The study did not involve minors. Data used for the study came from researchparticipants who were granted anonymity. These participants were assigned numerical identities for confidentiality and were paid for their participation. A second group involved psychology undergraduate students at three separate universities in the UnitedStates. Those students received course credit for participation. Theresearch team used these two cross-sectional samples and a 1- year longitudinal study.

"Collectively, these findings suggest that perceived addiction to Internet pornography, but not pornography use itself, is related to psychological distress, which runs counter to the narrative that many people have put forth. It doesn't seem to be the pornographyitself that is causing folks problems, it's how they feel about it," Grubbs said. Prior research by Grubbs and Exline has shown tha perceived addiction to Internet pornography is partially driven byreligious beliefs sand moral disapproval of pornography.

IMPLICATIONS OF PSYCHOLOGY

Early Years STEM Learning Emerging from the literature review, further research is likely to illuminate how different individuals respond to instruction during early years education. The literature review reveals the fact that children start school with potentially verydifferent levels of ability in some key areas that predict achievementin STEM subjects (including linguistic ability, quantitative ability,spatial ability and executive function). We are beginning tounderstand the way in which these skills combine to provide a foundation for STEM Learning, but in the future education is likely tobenefit from: Improved methods of identifying the individual needsof children. Tests for various abilities are already used in research, but these are not always convenient or appropriate to apply inclassroom practice.

This can be due to the time required to administer the tests, or to the need to administer them on a 1-to-1 basis. In the future, novel methods of measuring precursor abilities in classroom contexts,with good levels of reliability and validity, will provide schools and teachers with new and more effective methods by which to target differentiated support and instruction. Improved methods of supporting children with low levels of precursor skills and abilities. Given that these skills and abilities are strong predictors of future learning, it may be important that children identified as having low levels of particular abilities on entering formal education are supported in ways that focus on these abilities. Research cited I the literature review indicates some limited success has already been demonstrated in raising levels of these precursor skills, but further pursuit of research in this area will help identify more effective interventions for children with different levels of need and at different ages. Some research has already taken seriously the need to focus on individual differences in response to STEM instruction, and to explore interventions that can address diverse needs for support. An excellent example of this approach is Dowker's (2005a; 2005b) componential model of arithmetic, that led to the development of the Catch-Up Numeracy programme. This research was not included in the literature review as its theoretical basis appears more educational than psychological or neuroscientific. However it provides clear evidence that a focus on individual differences in children's learning can lead to improved outcomes. In the next 20 years,improved understanding of discrete predictors of achievement in STEM (e.g. spatial ability, quantitative ability, linguistic ability) and, perhaps more importantly, the ways in which they interact, will stimulate new insights into ways in which curriculum material can best be introduced, and new insights into ways in which material can be differentiated according to children's abilities.

PARENTAL MEDIATION OF DIGITAL USAGE

Most children of the current generation grow up in media-rich homes. Media are present in the majority of households and new technologies, such as tablets and smartphones, have emerged in Euro-American contexts. As indicated in a systematic review ofEuropean research (Ólafsson, Livingstone, & Haddon, 2013), mos research on children and digital media has focused on children aged 9 and above. However, due to the recent, rapid adoption of touch-screen devices most children use digital media and the internet at an earlier age (Findahl, 2013). Even children aged 3-4 use electronic gadgets and are avid users of technology (Ofcom, 2014). However, children are substantially influenced by their parents and their daily practices. Parental mediation is defined as the parental management of the relationship between children and media, including simple restrictions, conversational and interpretive strategies, and parental monitoring activities (Livingstone & Helsper,2008). Parental mediation is a key factor in the online lives of youngchildren; however, there is a dearth of research on the parental mediation of young children (Nikken & de Haan, 2015; Shin & Huh, 2011) and we do not know how parental mediation is related to specific risks and opportunities. We also lack a greater understanding of the role of children and their characteristics in the mediation process. Consistent with the new sociology of childhood (Christensen & James, 2008) we consider the child as an active subject who is not only formed by the system of family and exogenous factors, but also plays an active role in the construction of the family and its environment. Children are not passive recipients of parental mediation. They can influence the approachesby which their parents regulate their activities (Prout, 2008). Therefore, in the present research, we sought to understand how parents mediate the online experiences of young children in the family context, what is the role of the child in the mediation, and howparents mediate specific online risks and opportunities.

YOUNG CHILDREN'S ONLINE EXPERIENCES

To understand parenting in the digital age, it is necessary to understand young children's online behavior because the activitie that children engage in with digital technologies can lead to experiencing different kinds of outcomes. Findings related to negative experiences and outcomes (i.e., risks and harm) show thatchildren's technology use can be associated with content risks (e.g.,seeing upsetting pictures), contact risks (e.g., receiving unwanted messages from strangers), and conduct risks (e.g., online aggression) (Livingstone, Mascheroni, & Staksrud, 2017). Positive experiences and outcomes (i.e., opportunities and benefits) canalso be divided into the same broad areas: content (e.g., learning new information), contact (e.g., enhancing social competencies), and conduct (e.g., identity expressions).

The risks and opportunities for adolescents and youth are well-documented, and to some extent also for the population in middle childhood. There are wide national studies for these ages in the United States (Youth Internet Safety Survey, ages 10-17) and in Europe (EU Kids Online II and III, ages 9-16). They focus on the prevalence, related factors, associated risks and opportunities, and coping strategies for selected online activities. Research on younger children and their use of digital technology is more scarce and has only recently begun to expand; for example, recent research in the USA focuses on the role of media in children's development, especially in the context of education (e.g., Blackwell, Lauricella, & Wartella, 2014). However, most research has mainly been published in descriptive research reports (e.g., Chaudron et al.,2015; Rideout & Katz, 2016) or in reports that have a dominant focus on preschoolers (e.g., Marsh et al., 2015).

Research findings indicate that preschool children (Marsh et al., 2015) and children around 7 years old (Chaudron et al., 2015; Nikken & Jansz, 2014) are engaged in more limited online activities and thus are exposed to different risky situations than the olde population – such as different content that is evaluated as uncomfortable, or commercial risks. Children aged 8 and older progressively expand the range of their activities in comparison withyounger children (e.g., they start using social networking sites, play online games; Ofcom, 2016), which may lead to experiencing more varied risks as well as opportunities. New activities that children engage in represent unique experiences for children to cope with, but also pose a challenge for the whole family, which must dynamically react to the children's development.

PARENTAL MEDIATION

According to Youn (2008), parental mediation is a form of parental socialization because parents, as the primary socialization agents, influence their children's behaviors and attitudes to become more competent technology users. We defined parental mediation above as parental management of the relation between children and mediain line with Livingstone and Helsper (2008). Parental mediation could also be seen as a "specific" or "new" type of parenting. However, many different classifications of parental mediation have been formulated in previous studies (such as Nikken & Jansz, 2014;Zaman, Nouwen, Vanattenhoven, de Ferrerre, & Van Looy, 2016; Livingstone, Ólafsson, et al., 2017).

The first studies of parental mediation in children's television viewing identified three main types of parental mediation: active/instructive mediation, restrictive mediation, and co-viewing(Nathanson, 1999; Warren, 2003). Based on previous classifications, Livingstone and Helsper (2008) created four widely- used mediation types specifically for the mediation of children's digital media usage: active co-use, technical restrictions, interaction restrictions, and monitoring. The active co-use category suggest that sharing the media is more active when the child uses theinternet than when they watch television. It refers to behavior in which the parent is sitting near the child and talks to them about the online activity. Co-use also involves restrictions associated with the communication of personal information online, shopping online, completing forms, etc. These restrictions are included in this category because parents can explain and enforce such restrictions during co-use. Diverse restriction strategies were divided into two different categories: technical restrictions and interaction restrictions. The interaction-restriction category is associated with the prohibition of contacting others (e.g., using e-mail, chat, game playing). Technical restrictions represent the installation or use of software that, for example, filter content and prevent access tosome websites. The last category, parental monitoring, is connectedto checking the child's activities after the child's use of the internet, either covertly or overtly (Livingstone & Helsper, 2008).

The previous research on the styles of parental mediation wasmostly carried out among families with children 9 years old and older (i.e., Haddon, 2015; Talves & Kalmus, 2015). Research on families with younger children is more scarce. Research on themediation of younger children was carried out by Nikken and Jansz (2014) with Dutch parents of children aged 2 to 12. The authors revealed the following five mediation styles: co-use (e.g., using the internet together); active mediation (e.g., helping childrenunderstand what to do when being harassed online); restrictivemediation of access (e.g., general restrictions, time limitations); restrictive content-specific mediation (e.g., banning certain sites); and supervision (e.g., parent's monitoring of their children's internet use when nearby). The authors identify supervision as a new mediation in the context of online behavior. In contrast t Livingstone and Helsper (2008), Nikken and Jansz (2014) did not find monitoring the child's activities after the child's use of the internet to be a distinct type of mediation. They hypothesized that this kind of mediation applies more to older children.

Zaman et al. (2016) carried out a qualitative, mixed-method study inBelgium that included 24 Flemish parents and their 36 children, aged 3 to 9. They investigated the strategies the parents used to mediate their young children's media use and what contextual factors influenced the parental mediation practices. They identified the following parental mediation practices: restrictive mediation, participatory learning involving co-use plus active mediation, and distant mediation. Restrictions of activities in terms of time, device, content, location, and purchase were found. Two types of co-use emerged in the data when parents behaved as helpers or as buddies. Parents behaving as helpers guided their children when they learned how to use the medium or when problems with usage arose. Parents as buddies shared some media activities with their children purely for enjoyment. Active mediation included discussionsbetween the parents and their children. The distant mediation included "deference" when parents decide not to intervene and to respect the autonomy of their children, and "supervision", which is associated with situations where the parents allow their children to use digital technology independently but under close parental supervision.

Zaman et al. (2016) also revealed several external and internal contextual factors that are associated with parental mediation. Situational factors were related to weather, family composition and schedule, social contact, the disposition of media devices, and the architecture of the house. Internal factors were related to attitudes, digital media, health, and parenting. The authors describe ho parental mediation is changing in relation to the contextual demandsthat evolve over time (such as the popularity of devices) or vary between locations (such as less strict rules in the car).

In the present article, we follow this line of research on the situational factors of parental mediation. We aim to develop an understanding of specific parental mediations in relation to online opportunities and risks in the family context.

FACTORS ASSOCIATED WITH PARENTAL MEDIATION

Recent research has discovered several factors that are associated with the parental mediation of technology use. On the individual level, studies have indicated that parental mediation can be related to demographic variables, such as the age and gender of the parents (Kirwil, Garmendia, Garitaonandia, & Martínez Fernández, 2009; Sonck, Nikken, & de Haan, 2013); the parents' education (Kirwil et al., 2009); the age and gender of the children (Eastin, Greenberg, & Hofschire, 2006; Livingstone & Helsper, 2008); the household socioeconomic status (Livingstone & Helsper, 2008); andthe family size (Sonck et al., 2013). Parental mediation is alsoassociated with the parents' perceptions of their children's digital skills (Livingstone, Ólafsson, et al., 2017); the level of the child's (Lee & Chae, 2012) and the parents' media literacy (Mendoza, 2009); the level of the parents' digital skills (Livingstone & Helsper, 2008); the child's motivation to use media; the frequency of media use in the family (Lee & Chae 2007; Livingstone & Helsper, 2008); and the parents' views on the various effects of media content on their children (Sonck et al., 2013). On the socio-cultural level, studies have indicated that parental mediation of their children's internet use is affected by the culture of their country (i.e., countries'individualistic or collectivistic values; Kirwil, 2009) and thei country's level of welfare (Kalmus & Roosalu, 2012). These studies focused on factors associated with parental mediation and theywere based on investigations within families with children aged 9 and older.

The other relevant factors for families with younger children were investigated even less. One project researched 896 Dutch parentsof children under 7 and investigated which factors on both the sideof the child and the parent characteristics predicted mediation by the parent (Nikken & Schols, 2015). The authors revealed thatchildren's media use is predicted by the children's skills to use the media and the age of the child. Furthermore, parental mediation strategies depended on the parents' attitudes toward media. Finally,the authors revealed that mediation strategies varied among families with infants, toddlers, preschoolers, and early-childhoodchildren. The study indicated that parental mediation was also associated with the children's media skills and media activities.

RESEARCH GOALS

As we explained above, our research assumed that the child is an active subject in the family system and that the child plays an active role in the process of technology mediation. The role of youngchildren in the mediation process has not been sufficiently investigated in previous research and we aim to fill this gap with our research. In our investigation, we focus on the mediation strategies that parents use to shape the online experiences of 7-8-year-old children and we investigate the parental mediation of specific online opportunities and online risks for young children. We sought also to understand the situational factors that play a role in the parental mediation of technology risks and opportunities, and the active role of the child from the perspective of the parents

METHOD PARTICIPANTS

The sample consisted of 10 families from the Czech Republic (N_{mother} = 8, N_{father} = 6, $N_{children}$ = 21) who had at least one 7-8-year- old child (N = 10, M = 7.5 years SD = 0.39) who used a tablet, PC,or smartphone at least once a week. The parents' ages ranged from35 to 41. For detailed information see Table 1. Seven families had two parents; three had a single parent (a mother); and one family shared their household with a grandfather. All of the parents were Czech. Their education ranged from vocational to university level. The income of the families also varied from under half of the national median to above the national median. All the families had PC/laptops, smartphones, and mobile phones in the household.Seven families owned at least one tablet. The children had accessto these devices. Some children had possession of their own devices (specified in Table 1). Within this research, we analyzed data from interviews with parents.

PROCEDURE

Our research was part of a research project called "Young Children (0-8) and Digital Technology" carried out by the Joint Research Centre, Institute for the Protection and Security of the Citizen (see Chaudron et al., 2015). The present research is based on a more detailed re-analysis of the data collected in the Czech Republic only. Individual face-to-face interviews — separately with the parent(s) and separately with the child/children — were carried out from September 2014 to October

2014. Interviews took place in the home of the participants. The semi-structured interviews with parents were between 35 and 85 minutes long (60 minutes onaverage). Parents were interviewed about four main areas: (1 devices employed, activities, and skills; (2) parental mediation; (3) family rules about technology usage; and (4) the parents' perceptions of new technologies and parental concerns of technologies. The interviewers used an interview guide to follow questions and observation protocol as developed by the Joint Research Centre (for detailed information, see Chaudron et al.,2015).

To find participants, six primary schools in the South Moravia regionwere sent a request to forward invitations for participation to students of second-year classes, which were then delivered to parents. Approximately 350 invitations were distributed in this way. Thirty families registered to participate in the study and interviews were subsequently held in 10 of them. Families where chosen to create a variable sample – in order to have two- and one-parent families; to have families with one and more children; to have families with child/children who owned a device on their own etc. The parents received gifts for their children provided by the Joint Research Centre and 1,000 CZK (approximately 37 EUR) for participating in the research (the national median monthly incomefor a two-member family is 24,000 CZK, approximately 888 EUR).

All of the participants were informed about the purpose of the research and they provided written informed consent. The study received ethical approval from the European Commission. For moreinformation, see the general report from all seven countries (Chaudron et al., 2015)

ANALYSES

All interviews were transcribed verbatim. For the purpose of this study, only interviews with parents were analyzed. A Thematic Analysis procedure was applied as the analytic method (Braun & Clarke, 2006). The first and second authors conducted theanalyses. The six steps of the Thematic Analysis method wereused:

- getting familiar with the data through multiple readings of the transcripts in an excel file
- generating initial codes to highlight topics in the data
- grouping the codes into categories and searching for recurring themes
- reviewing the emergent themes
- defining and naming the themes
- producing the report (Braun & Clarke, 2006)

To increase the validity of the findings and to strengthen the inter- coder triangulation of results, an audit was completed. The third author validated the themes developed by the first and secondauthors.

RESULTS

The parents of 7-8-year-old children face the necessity of using mediation strategies for technology usage. We describe three themes (see Table 2) related to the mediation strategies of parents:
1. Mediation strategies of technology usage;
2. Time and place management of mediation strategies; and
3. Child as a co-creator of mediation strategies

MEDIATION STRATEGIES OF TECHNOLOGY USAGE

Families in our sample reported mediation strategies for general technology usage and mediation strategies in the context of specifictechnology opportunities and risks. Two subthemes were identified:

(A) the mediation of technology opportunities, and (B) the future mediation of technology risks.
Mediation strategies for general technology usage are related more to general rules and beliefs than to specific risks and opportunities. The parents' mediation strategies for young children are often linkedto the belief that children are too young and they do not do inappropriate things with technologies, such as communicating with strangers or finding inappropriate content. As one family (C5) reveals: Father: "For now they are visiting just appropriate sites, for now theyare not going elsewhere, but we will see how it will be in the future. (…) such as they could find websites that are not for them where is… Mother: …where is some advertisement and she [daughter, 7 years old] will click on it and there will be a porn site or something. (…) Father: But now it is ok, we are waiting [for what will be in the future].

The majority of the families do not have strict rules for technology usage. Those families usually set rules situationally: "I never really had the intention to set [rules], because sometimes he doesn't even touch it and sometimes he sits there for a bit longer, for example. But it is not really like – well now you have an hour. I never really, I never intend to impose it" (Mother, C10). Technology usage in such families was perceived to be one of many activities. Therefore, the did not have any special rules. Nevertheless, general rules were applied. For example, free-time activities (including technologies) were allowed after chores and schoolwork were completed, and children had to request permission to use technologies.

Some of the families had strict rules. These rules related to the time spent with technologies and to the more accurate control of technology usage. Some parents set up rules specifically for technologies that were perceived as something special. For example, in some families technology usage was a form   of reward or punishment:

"Anyway, for a reward, and when there is time, that means when… they have a lot of free-time activities, so when we come home, the first thing is to do the homework. When they are finished with the homework and there is time left and there were no problems at school, then there is some kind of reward" (Father, C2).

Mediation strategies for specific opportunities and risks were also identified. Parents reported (a) co-use – the parent uses technology together with the child; (b) active mediation – the parent explain issues related to technology; (c) supervision – the child uses technologies while a parent is nearby; (d) parent as role model – theparent use technology while the child is observing the parent'sactivities; (e) restrictive mediation – the parent set up restrictions in the context of technology usage; and (f) trial and error – the parent knowingly lets the child use trial and error while using technology. The next two subthemes describe the content of the parental mediation – the mediation of opportunities and the mediation   ofrisks as perceived by the parents. That means that the parents themselves linked some of their specific mediation activities to the opportunities, such as digital skills or possible risks. We believe it I important to clarify what the goal is for these mediation activities from the parental perspective, especially because parents are very active only in the mediation of opportunities and almost completely inactive in the mediation of risks, as we show below.

Mediation of technology opportunities. Parents from our sample gave extensive examples that provided insight   into their mediation of technology opportunities. Technology opportunities perceived by parents for children include free-time activities, practical technology usage, and educational purposes. Parents also mentioned digital skills that children could learn/improve during all of the above- mentioned opportunities. In terms of the mediation strategies of online opportunities, from parent reports we identified the following strategies: co-use, active mediation, supervision, parent as role model, and restrictive mediation, and some parents let their childrenlearn themselves by trial and error.

Digital skills. Trial and error was linked to digital skills. Someparents let their children learn to use technologies themselves, like how to download applications, and use them: "Intuitively. Trial and error, so it is not like it would be targeted… she   tries   it herself" (Mother, C10). Co-use was also used to manage digital skills. This strategy was initiated by either the children or the parents. Some parents pointed out that their children ask how to continue a game, and they ask for help when they can not read or speak the language. As a father (C8) explained: "They [daughter, 7 years old, and son, 10 years old] could download games on their own, (…) when the game asked for some information they asked what to do and we [father and mother] told them." Co-use initiatedby parents was linked to active mediation when parents explain, for example, how to use PC components, like a mouse or a keyboard and how bookmarks, browsers, and some applications work. As a father (C4) pointed out:

"I showed him that he has a bookmark there. Then when he wantsto look at something, there it is. And then I saved him tutorials for rubber-band knitting [a popular activity for children in the Czech Republic] into the bookmarks. I told him that he does not need to look for it, he does not need to google it. It is just enough to open it in the bookmark bar. He knows that now."

Parents as role models improves digital skills because it allows children to observe their parents' technology usage. Parents motivate their children to use technologies in the same way as they use them: "Otherwise, he, of course, sees us working, so for example when they are waiting for when a person finishes   their work and lets them go on the internet, they see part of the work" (Mother, C3).

Free-time activities. Supervision is usually applied during free-timeactivities when children are allowed to use technology while   a parent is nearby. Co-use is also part of some free-time activities, such as playing games or watching videos. Free-time activities,especially games, are a part of the restrictive mediation, such as when some parents control games. As a father (C2) reflected: "So we need to choose, select, what is a suitable game for [my son]."

Practical technology usage. Parents also mentioned teaching children how technologies can help them in everyday life. They try to show children the available possibilities, like different programs and websites that could help people connect their online and offline lives, such as when they search the family vacation together. Parents usually use active mediation in combination with co-use while they search for timetables (e.g., so children get to school o their own), vacation destinations (e.g., show pictures of places and the possibilities for how to get there), free-time activities (e.g., websites of different free-time activity clubs), and shop online. For example, a father (C5) described how they look for free-time activities in their family (daughters 5 and 7 years old): "…photos andalso the virtual tours are really great… for example, Wikyland [Child Park]. So we just looked, how it looks there, so we looked at the photos – Yeah, we want to go there [the daughters said]."

Education. For educational purposes, parents usually use co-useor supervision to mediate some (school) activities, such as to learn reading, writing, and mathematical skills, as a father (C5) reveals: "When she [daughter, 7 years old] was younger, she learned how towrite, she liked it. We opened Word and I told her 'A' and she found and wrote 'A', and then she tried to write also whole words." Parentsalso mentioned that some games could improve their children's language knowledge and also basic economics skills, like profits and losses in games, or social skills, like fair play, or how to take care of someone. A mother (C9) talked about an educational program on a CD that her son used to learn languages while she supervised the process: "[My son, 8 years old] learns Czech language and English. He had this CD, there are some assignmentsand when he fills them in he goes to the next level and he travels around the world."

Future mediation of technology risks. Parents reported knowledge about technology risks, such as internet overuse, game addiction, meeting unknown people online (i.e., stranger danger, pedophiles), cyberbullying, data misuse, and inappropriate content. Nevertheless, every parent in our sample perceived those risks as not yet present and the use of mediation strategies unnecessary for young children. As a mother (C5) reported "Now we really cannot do anything, because like my husband says, they are not at the stage when they would have some need forsocial networking sites, so there is no point in telling them. Now we tell them not to sit in a car with a stranger after school. We don't jumble their minds with the internet."

This do-nothing strategy could also be linked to the belief thatmediation strategies will only be needed when something happens: "I deal with things when they come. Like, I don't worry about something that is not an issue. I try not to forbid something that has not yet happened" (Mother, C1). So far, parents   wait and do not pay attention to this potential problem. For   every parent in our sample, technology risks for their children in the future were connected to social networking sites (SNS). Two parents revealed that they do not want their children to know that SNS exists. Theytry to avoid the sites as long as possible, and they would rather lie about their SNS use than explain it. Other parents linked the start oftechnology risks with the development of reading and social skills, and the necessity to increase technology usage because of schoolwork.

Parents expect to deal with those risks in the future when thechildren start to visit SNS and develop an online social life. For example, a father (C8) shared his fear of cyberbullying: "We are probably afraid of contacts with different people on social sites, but we are afraid maybe more of bullying or cyberbullying thanof contacts with older people with the inclination to pedophilia. Not that, I don't think so. I think that our children are cautious enough."

Another father (C2) shared his struggles about the mediation of danger from contact with strangers. Once he tried to talk about it with his 8-year-old son, but he did not know how and he found I difficult to use appropriate language and not scare him; therefore,he had not yet done it:

"Here you have a person, a small child, second grade, so how to tellhim this fact about these people that abuse children or they pretend to be someone else... And at the same time it is probably difficult to do it in a way the child can understand, that things like this happen, and that it can be unpleasant, but at the same time not to scarethem with something that it is dreadful."

Parents differ about the strategies for how to mediate those risks in the future. Some parents do not yet know how they will manage it. Others would like to use mediation strategies that they already knowfrom the offline world, and apply them to the online environment, i.e.the mediation of meeting strangers in the offline world applies similarly in the online one. Some parents also rely on school and theschools' technology risk-mediation programs. However,   everyparent agreed that the mediation of technology risks will be necessary in the future.

TIME AND PLACE MANAGEMENT OF MEDIATION STRATEGIES

Time and place management of mediation strategies are important parts of the mediation process of technology usage. Parents reported that they distinguish between free time and working time. Mediation can be different on weekends, during holidays and days off, and during school days. As a father (C5) expressed: "During holidays, there is more freedom but during the school year... when the older daughter comes home from school, first she has to do the homework and only after that she can play." The time of day also made a difference in the mediation process. Some families set up rituals related to the daytime and nighttime. For example, watchin fairy tales before bedtime or using technologies while the   parent was walking the dog in the morning.

There are also changes for exceptional occasions, like traveling, a doctor visit, an illness, or bad weather. As a mother (C10) remarked: "These mobile phones, during travelling when there are long periods of waiting, then there (we use them)." Exceptions may also be made for visits by friends and a family member, like grandparents who may apply different mediation strategies than the parents. Another special occasion is when the parents need time fortheir own work and they required the children to be engaged and to entertain themselves. Technologies are perceived as helpful in suchoccasional situations. As a mother (C10) reflected: "At home, when Ineed to do something quickly and I need to somehow, like, put her away.   When   I say it bluntly, it really is for putting her away." Additionally, special occasions are also related to situations when children are alone, such as when they go to school or to a free-time activity. During such situations parents perceived smartphones as a communication and a monitoring tool to stay in touch with their children. This motivation is pivotal for some parents: "That is why I bought him the mobile phone, so I could control him when he would sometimes go with a friend and now I could just call him to check and know where he is" (Mother, C6). Nevertheless, when children have their own smartphones they also have the opportunity to use them without parental supervision. Consequently, these occasions usually lead to a more liberal mediation strategy, where children are not adequately controlled, or no mediation strategy. Parents let their children use technologies bythemselves, sometimes without supervision, during exceptional occasions like an illness or while parents are working or doing household chores. As a mother pointed out (C9): "I can use the P to let them watch something so they would not be scared while I go out for a walk with the dog."

We can conclude that situational factors in the mediation process are strong. Parental mediation strategies are co-constructed by parents and their children and are changing according to the specific family situation. The mediation of technology is not a stable parental behavior, but it is always developing and changing in context, according to time, place, and the children's characteristics and behavior.

CHILD AS A CO-CREATOR OF MEDIATION STRATEGIES

The parents' perceptions of their children's approaches to technologies seem to be important aspects of the mediation strategies. We identified three relevant subthemes of this category:
(A) technologies as a natural part of the child's environment,
(B) thechild's interactions with the parents, and
(C) the   parent's perceptions of their child`s reaction to technology usage.

Technologies as a natural part of the child's environment. The parents in our sample reported that children behave naturally and spontaneously with respect to technologies, and that technologies are a natural part of their everyday lives. They naturally   learn quickly by observation and imitation. They quickly develop digital skills and use technologies on their own. For instance, a father (C2) said: "The children, they perceive it differently from the grownups, naturally right. When I show them something, they take it completelynaturally and they are not learning, they just see it and that is how they do it." Such an approach encourages parents to perceive technologies as an important part of the everyday lives of their children. Parents think that children are learning naturally from observing other people. They believe that these abilities will help them in the future to use technologies properly.

The child's interactions with the parents. Parents appreciated that their children communicated with them about their technology usage. This subtheme is linked to some mediation strategies, namely co-use initiated by children and parent as role model. Parents reported that their children were able to ask for help when they struggled while using technology, and they asked for permission to use technology. As a father (C4) reported: "Every timethere is some kind of problem or when he needs help with something, he comes to me. He just comes to me and asks." Parents as role models reported that their children also liked to observe their technology usage to learn new things. Consequently, parents reported that their children shared their curiosity and had a tendency to ask questions about several topics connected to the technologies. These strategies soothe parents. Parents trust their children and rely on their ability to ask for help.

The parent´s perceptions of their child`s reaction to technologyusage. Two approaches were identified within the third subtheme:
(a) technology usage is perceived by parents as one of many activities, and
(b) technology usage is perceived by parents as the preferred activity of the child.

Technology usage is perceived by parents as one of many activities. Some parents reported their children's technology usage in the context of many other activities, such as sports, games with friends, outdoor activities, and hobbies. Parents also talked about their children's tendency to follow rules and make compromises. Some children are, according to their parents, able to stop using technologies by themselves or when asked to. Parents als perceived that some children spend an acceptable amount of time suitable amount of time with technologies, and they like also other offline activities as well. Technologies are "just" another option of many activities. As a mother (C9) put it: "I was surprised, my daughter [6 years old] is not envious that her brother [8 years old] already has a mobile phone. She is active herself. She is drawing, playing with dolls...she had more activities than technologies." Some parents reported that they have a tendency to set less rules or no specific rules at all. For example, children spendan acceptable amount of time   on technologies by themselves, so the parents do not need to set time restrictions. Some parentsbelieved their children behave responsible. As a father (C5) reported: "During the school year, the older daughter is so responsible that she deleted the games where you have to take care of animals. That means, she uninstalled them... and when the holidays come she will install them again so she will have time for them."

Technology usage is perceived by parents as the preferred activity. In comparison to previous category, other parents have different experiences with children. These parents perceived their children to be unable to stop the activity themselves or even when asked to. Sometimes they talked about potential tendencies to addiction or they reported that their children were fascinated by technologies. That means that their children would like to use technology any time when it is possible: "I have a feeling with [my son] that he is more inclined to habits... when he plays these gamesit can be on any device, he has trouble detaching from   it, and he can spend endless time with it" (Father, C2). For these children, parents reported the tendency to set more rules and control more media usage. Some parents remarked that they talked with thei children and explained things to them, such as the difference between fiction and reality.

The parents of three families reported having one child who was fascinated by the technologies and another who balanced technology usage with other activities. These parents distinguished those two preferences and had the tendency to compare their children. They are able to mediate each child in a different way according to that child's habits with technology preference. As the mother (C3) pointed out: "As far as computers are concerned, a tendency of almost addictionappeared with [my older son – 7 years old]. Like, from early ages hewas fascinated. And, for example, the younger son [3 years old] does not have it at all. There I don't have the need to look at it as closely, because when he, for example, watches or does somethingon the computer for a while, then he comes to me and says that he had enough."

DISCUSSION

Our study contributes to the current stage of knowledge of theparental mediation of technology risks with in-depth qualitative insight and focus on the situational factors in families with children aged 7-8. Our findings indicate that the parental mediation of digital media is a dynamic process that is co-constructed by the parents and the children in the context of the actual situation.

In the next three sections, we discuss our findings concerning the mediation strategies of online opportunities and risks, the time and place management of mediation strategies as a factor related to parental mediation, and the child as a co-creator of mediation strategies

MEDIATION STRATEGIES OF TECHNOLOGY USAGE

Our results suggest that parents use various kinds of mediation strategies, such as co-use, active mediation, supervision, parent as role model, restrictive mediation, and trial and error. Similar types ofparental mediations have already been identified by previous research (Nikken & Jansz, 2014; Zaman et al., 2016). In our investigation, we enrich current knowledge by linking these mediation strategies to specific online opportunities and risks. We believe this distinction between the different goals of the mediation strategies is important because our results have revealed that parents in our sample mostly mediate the digital opportunities and do almost no mediation of the online risks for young children. Our analyses demonstrate only the perspectives of parents, such as the parents saying that the "trial and error" mediation is linked to opportunities because "children are learning on their   own". However, it is clear that such an approach of parents might be problematic because children who learn on their own are also endangered by several online risks (Nikken & Jansz, 2014; Smahel,Wright, & Cernikova, 2014), but parents did not acknowledge this problem with self-learning in our research. In the virtual environment, the border between online opportunities and risks is more blurred than it is reported by the parents in our study, who mainly described the mediation of online opportunities. Future research may reflect the possible consequences of this "trial and error" approach, such as the relation to possible online risks that children could experience while learning on their own.

The mediation of technology opportunities was mostly connected to "content opportunities" where parents let children learn new things and let them improve their digital skills. Digital skills are mediated bydifferent approaches, such as co-use, active mediation, and paren as role model. Contact opportunities that were identified in the previous research on older children were not directly present in our results. Some parents used games or programs in the educational context, which could improve some aspects of their children's socialskills, such as fair play. Parents also did not mention any conduct opportunities for their children. This could be linked to the characteristics of their children's activities. Children in our sampledo not participate in SNS, blogs, or online games. Parents also did not mention these applications as possible opportunities in the future.

Concerning the mediation of online risks for young children,   it seems that parents in our sample underestimated the possible online risks. The parents were mostly afraid of the "contact risk", such as the possibility that their children could communicate with strangers online, like within social networking sites. Therefore, it seems that parents from our sample were mostly afraid of thefuture, which is in line with the study carried out in Singapore on the population of families with children aged 7 to 12 (Shin, 2015). But previous research has also indicated that young children (under 8 years old) are sometimes exposed to interactions with online strangers within online games (Brito & Dias, 2016). Parents in our sample were not aware of this problem and they planned to mediateonline risks in the future when their young children start to communicate more online. Future research should investigate this issue on larger samples and in more cross-cultural contexts.

Further, within our sample none of the parents spoke about the "content risk", such as advertising, violent content, sexual content, or idealized thin or muscular images that can be displayed to children on the internet (Staksrud & Livingstone, 2009). For instance, media exposure of the ideal physique could be linked wit some eating disorders symptomatology, mostly among users at risk for developing an eating disorder (Hausenblas et al., 2013). It seems that parents in our sample underestimate this kind of risk. In the previous research, about 10% of parents reported that their children under 5 years old had made in-app purchases by accident and that children had been exposed to content that made them feel uncomfortable (Marsh et al., 2015). This theme requires furtherresearch that should involve more methods, such as recording the screen devices of children. It is evident that some parents do not know about inappropriate content and further research should probably directly investigate the online behavior of children.

The parents in our sample also did not speak about the possible "conduct risk" where the child becomes an actor within possibly risky scenarios, such as creating aggressive content, and harassingor bullying others (Staksrud & Livingstone, 2009). However, Marsh (2010) reported these kinds of behaviors within the virtual world among 5-8-year-old children, such as throwing virtual snowballs at avatars, excluding avatars from parties, and name-calling. It seems that parents are not aware that their children aged 7 and 8 might engage in this type of possibly risky behavior.

In our investigation, parents reported almost no mediation strategiesrelated to online risks, but they reported many strategies for enriching their children's opportunities, such as digital skills. The enrichment of digital skills might lead to better resilience against online risks. Vandoninck and d'Haenens (2014) reported that technical instrumental actions, such as deleting, unfriending, or blocking certain people, might lead to successful preventivestrategies against online risks.

Time and Place Management of Mediation Strategie Time and place was described by parents as a very important factorfor the mediation itself. This result is in line with the research of Zaman et al. (2016), who also indicated the importance of considering contextual factors, like when, where, and under which external conditions children are allowed to use the media. Several studies have shown that parents use rules to mediate their children's usage (i.e., Livingstone & Helsper, 2008). Our study indicates that rules are not strict in some families, and that the rules are set more situationally in relation to the context, such as where and when the children use the technology and also what the needs of the parents are. Therefore, some parents are not able to report specific rules of technology usage that are more contextual and theyrely on general rules that are valid for both offline and online life, such as when children finish their homework they can play their dolls or the tablet.

Our results indicate that parental mediation strategies change according to the family situation. They are not a stable, easily measurable behavior; rather, they emerge over and over againaccording to time, place, and the parents' and children's characteristics and behavior. Up-to-date research has mostly measured the socio-demographic factors of parents and children that impact parental mediation, such as gender, age, education, digital skills (i.e., Livingstone, Ólafsson, et al., 2017; Nikken & Schols, 2015). We suggest that future research should involve the context of the situation more, such as the time and place of the application of the mediation strategies, because there is nothing likestable general mediation. Therefore, we recommend that future surveys should not only ask about general parental mediation but also connect the mediation to a concrete situation and context.Future research should also reflect the role of the parents perceptions of their children's behavior, such as their ability to ask for help. When parents, for example, believe that their children will ask them for help if a problem occurs, they apply fewer mediation strategies than if they believe their children will not ask for help. Thesituational factors, such as the time and place management ofmediation strategies, also play a role in the possible underestimation of online risks because, in certain situations, such as travelling and when parents need time for themselves, parents apply fewer mediation strategies or they do not use mediation strategies at all.

CHILD AS A CO-CREATOR OF MEDIATION STRATEGIES

According to Mesch (2009), the research of parental mediation was based on the premise that technologies can affect children's attitudes and behaviors. These technological effects can beinfluenced by parental activities to a certain extent. Nevertheless, our research indicated that parents are also influenced by their child's behavior, which then affected their mediation strategies. In our perception, parental mediation is more a process of the interactions between children and parents that co-constructs the mediation strategies of the parents. The reported parental perceptions of children as the co-creators of the mediation strategies is in line with the new sociology of childhood (Christensen& James, 2008), which presents the child as an adequate socialization agent and not just the recipient of parental care. Although our research is from the parental perspective, the parents acknowledge the role of their children in the mediation process. Thisresult also supports the study of Livingstone, Ólafsson, et al. (2017),which indicates that the parental mediation of technology usage is interconnected with the parents' perception of their child's digital skills. When parents perceive a child as a competent internet use they support their activities, such as allowing them to use the technology for a longer time and without constant supervision. On the other hand, parents applied more restrictive strategies for less digitally skilled children which may further limit their possibilities for increasing digital skills. Future research should also reflect this position and should be focused on the different aspects of the child's behavior and the various factors that impact the parental mediation.

LIMITATIONS AND FUTURE RESEARCH

Our investigation was carried out within only 10 families in theCzech Republic and the generalization of the results is very limited. We endeavored to make the sample various and we included families in different configurations (see Table 1). The nature of the sample allowed us an in-depth exploration of the families where children have regular access to technologies. Unfortunately, we do not know how it works in families with no regular access to technologies. We also did not have a family with young children whouse social networking sites in our sample. It may be that families with such young children use different mediation strategies becausesome parents said that they will use different strategies in the future when their children meet people online, such as within social networking sites. It is also possible that the parental mediationstrategies of young children's technology usage varies across countries and cultures. We recommend future quantitative and comparative research to validate such hypotheses. Our investigation was also focused only on the perspectives of parents, which is a substantial limitation. It might be that children would bringdifferent perspectives to the investigation.

Implication

Our research indicates that parental mediation is a dynamic processthat is co-constructed by the parents and the child in the context of the actual situation. This could indicate that it might be more effective to give education concerning digital skills to both parents and children together, such as in families and/or through online courses, because such education would affect both of the actors within the mediation process. It is also important to recognize that there is typically not one parental mediation strategy, but the strategies vary according to different situations. The "optimal mediation" could vary at different places (such as at home, onvacation, while travelling, or with grandparents) and at differenttimes (during weekdays, during weekends, or during holidays). The future education should be aware of these different contexts andthis knowledge could also be applied to educational programs for children, parents (Cook, 2016) and teachers (Karaseva, Siibak, Pruulmann-Vengerfeldt, 2015). For example, it could be recommended that parents should think more about the mediationof situations where they have less control over their children's technology usage, such as when the child is with grandparents or atsummer camps. Parents should speak with other caregivers about their mediation strategies to balance the approaches of both sides, or at least to know the mediation strategy of the other side.

It seems from our investigation that parents prefer to not speak with their young children about online risks. Parents should be informed about the possible online risks for their children, such as the contentor contact risks within online games. It might also be important to inform parents that they can help children to avoid risks by teaching their children digital skills.

EMERGING AREAS MCQS

1. Coronary artery disease (CAD) canbe determined by this test
(a) Cardiac catherization
(b) Electrocardiogram
(c) Treadmill stress test
(d) all of these
Answer: (d)

2. The modifiable risk factor associated with coronary arterydisease is
(a) Age
(b) Obesity
(c) Heredity
(d) Gender
Answer: (b)

3. This is one of the symptoms ofCoronary artery disease
(a) Sleep problems
(b) Headache
(c) Diarrhoea
(d) Pain or discomfort in the chest,lower jaw or arms
Answer: (d)

4. If a stent is not used in a few caseswho have coronary angioplasty done, the artery tends to narrow down or get blocked again in 6 months. This is more likely to happen if:
(a) one smokes

(b) one has unstable angina beforethe procedure
(c) one has diabetes
(d) all of these
Answer: (d)

5. Coronary angioplasty, part ofCAD's treatment involves:
(a) A new part of artery replaces theblocked section
(b) to expand artery, medication isused
(c) inflation of a tiny balloon insidean artery
(d) None of these
Answer: (c)

6. Doctors place a stent inside the artery during angioplasty. A stent is a
(a) A new fragment of the artery
(b) A wire mesh tube
(c) A cotton tube
(d) A slow-release medicine capsule
Answer: (b)

7. The_ branches into Circumflex artery and left anteriordescendary artery
(a) Left main coronary artery
(b) right marginal artery
(c) Posterior descendary artery
(d) None of these
Answer: (a)

8. One of these is not a symptom ofacute coronary syndrome
(a) ST Segment elevation myocardialinfarction
(b) Non ST segment elevationmyocardial infarction
(c) unstable angina
(d) No episodes of dyspnea
Answer: (d)

9.   Ischemia is
(a)   restriction of blood supply totissues
(b)   Overflow of blood to tissues
(c)   Inadequate deoxygenated bloodcarrying veins
(d)   the medical term for shortness of breath
Answer: (a)

10.   This is the role of the coronaryartery
(a) to carry blood away from the heart muscles
(b) to supply blood to heart muscles
(c) to supply blood to all parts of thebody
(d) none of these
Answer: (b)

11.person who incites or abets the commission of a crime andis present actually or constructively is considered tobe a(n):
(a) accessory before the fact
(b) principal in the first degree
(c) accessory after the fact
(d) principal in the second degree
Answer: (d)

12.   Which of the following is truein regard to conspiracy?
(a) Conspiracy permits criminal prosecution for the behavior of others as well as for one's own acts
(b) Conspiracy is a very importanttool for prosecutors
(c) Conspiracy may be distinguished from attempt in that attempt requires an act or preparation, whereas the agreementmay
   be sufficient to constitute the act requirement in conspiracy

(d) All of these are true

Answer: (d)

13. Which of the following is trueof forfeitures?

(a) RICO is the only federal statute that permits forfeitures

(b) RICO is used frequently as abasis for civil cases because of thepotentially high penalties

(c) Individuals who lose propertythrough forfeiture laws are always charged with crimes

(d) All of these are true

Answer: (b)

14. Which of the following is an example of an inchoate crime?

(a) attempt

(b) murder

(c) rape

(d) forgery

Answer: (a)

15. Which of the following is trueof solicitation?

(a) The incitement may bedirected at a crowd, not just aparticular individual

(b) Solicitation requires a purpose to promote or facilitate thecommission of a crime

(c) In some states renouncing thesolicitation is permitted as a defense to solicitation

(d) All of these are true

Answer: (d)

16. _crimes are important not only because they are threatening in and of themselves, but also because they may lead to other crimes.

(a) Strict liability

(b) Conspiracy

(c) Inchoate

(d) Petty

Answer: (c)

17. Enticing another person to commit a crime is known as:

(a) conspiracy

(b) solicitation

(c) aiding and abetting

(d) vicarious liability

Answer: (b)

18. A(n)____ crime is defined as an act involving two basic elements: a step toward the commissionof a crime and a specific intentto commit that crime.

(a) conspiracy

(b) inchoate

(c) strict liability

(d) attempt

Answer: (d)

19. To______is toassist or facilitate the commission of a crime.

(a) aid and abet

(b) conspire

(c) attempt

(d) coerce

Answer: (a)

20. Which of the following is a defense in an attempt case?

(a) impossibility

(b) renunciation

(c) incompleteness

(d) degree of seriousness

Answer: (a)

21. Some state legislatures have enacted statutes criminalizingthe knowing exposure of another to:
(a) syphilis
(b) herpes
(c) HIV or AIDS
(d) All of these are included inthe statutes
Answer: (c)

22. _________meansagreeing with another to join together for the purpose of committing an unlawful act oragreeing to use unlawful means to commit an act that would otherwise be lawful.
(a) Attempt
(b) Conspiracy
(c) Aid and abet
(d) Coercion
Answer: (b)

23. _________was intended by Congress to reachserious cases—major violatorswho engage in a pattern of racketeering activity.
(a) The Wharton rule
(b) Forfeiture
(c) The Pinkerton rule
(d) RICO
Answer: (d)

24.____means association in a wrongful act.
(a) Negligence
(b) Mens rea
(c) Complicity
(d) Tort
Answer: (c)

25. Under the common law a(n) _____________________was theperson who committed the crime.
(a) accessory
(b) principal
(c) accomplice
(d) co-conspirator
Answer: (b)

26. In recent years the U.S. Department of Justice has indicted_ who, they allege, have engaged in aiding and abetting or conspiring with their clients.
(a) attorneys
(b) doctors
(c) psychologists
(d) accountants
Answer: (a)

27. The_____rule is alimitation on parties to the crime of conspiracy.
(a) accomplice
(b) principal
(c) facilitation
(d) Wharton
Answer: (d)

28. Which of the following doesRICO prohibit?
(a) conducting or participating inan enterprise's affairs through a pattern of racketeering activity
(b) possession of marijuana
(c) prostitution
(d) treason

Answer: (a)

29. The_____holds that a co-conspirator may be held accountable for the acts of fellow conspirators even though the requirements of criminal culpability for the acts of accomplices are not met.
(a) Pinkerton rule
(b) Wharton rule
(c) husband-and-wife rule
(d) two-or-more rule
Answer: (a)

30. _is the taking by the government of money, personal items, or assets that were secured fromcriminal acts.
(a) Racketeering
(b) Confiscation
(c) Arbitration
(d) Forfeiture
Answer: (d)

31. Which of the following laws have been attacked as permitting police to exercise too much discretion, leading to discrimination against racialand ethnic minorities and the homeless?
(a) Fighting words
(b) Vagrancy
(c) Public intoxication
(d) Unlawful assembly
Answer: (b)

32. Which crime has been accepted as inevitable, evenessential, and in some societies esteemed?
(a) Fornication
(b) Seduction
(c) Lewdness
(d) Prostitution
Answer: (d)

33. Under common law, _______________refers to the meeting of three or morepersons to disturb the public peace, with the intention of participating in a forcible andviolent execution of an unlawful enterprise or of a lawful enterprise in an unauthorized manner.
(a) Rout
(b) Riot
(c) Unlawful assembly
(d) Public disturbance
Answer: (c)

34. Which of the following is *not* true regarding childpornography?
(a) In 2002, the U.S. Supreme Court held that virtual child pornography—that which is created by computer simulations—may be owned or sold without violating federal statutes
(b) Congress and many states have enacted statutes aimed solely at child pornography
(c) All Judges support increased sentences for those in possession of child pornography
(d) The federal statute concerning child pornography provides for forfeiture of any property or proceeds obtained, used, or produced as a result of the crime committed
Answer(c)

35. Which of the following crimeshas been declared unconstitutional in many jurisdictions?
(a) Disorderly conduct
(b) Vagrancy
(c) Disturbing the peace
(d) Minor is possession
Answer: (b)

36. ________is a willfully committed act that disturbs the public tranquility or order and for which there isno legal justification.
(a) Pandering

(b) Riot
(c) Breach of the peace
(d) Disorderly conduct
Answer: (c)

37. Which of the following crimeshas been declared unconstitutional in many jurisdictions?
(a) Disorderly conduct
(b) Vagrancy
(c) Disturbing the peace
(d) Minor is possession
Answer: (b)

38. _refers to the act by a man who uses solicitation, persuasion, promises, bribes, or other methods to entice a woman tohave unlawful sexual intercourse with him.
(a) Pandering
(b) Fornication
(c) Lewdness
(d) Seduction
Answer: (d)

39. Which of the following involves a minor offense, suchas drunkenness or fighting?
(a) Pandering
(b) Disorderly conduct
(c) Vagrancy
(d) Loitering
answer: (b)

40. Another word for panderingis:
(a) Pimping
(b) Bribery
(c) Prostitution
(d) Embezzlement
Answer: (a)

41. ________is consensual sexual intercoursebetween a married person
(a) Fighting words
(b) Vagrancy
(c) Adultery
(d) Fornication
Answer: (c)

42. Which of the following is notan alcohol and drug related offense discussed in the textbook?
(a) Drug abuse
(b) Public intoxication
(c) Driving Under the Influence
(d) Minor in possession
Answer: (a)

43. Under common law, unlawfulassembly was considered a___.
(a) Felony
(b) Violation
(c) Misdemeanor
(d) Violent crime
Answer: (c)

44. Historically, offenses against and someone other than his or___________encompasses acts her spouse.
(a) Public decency
(b) Public order

(c) Public morality

(d) Society

Answer: (a)

45. Which of the following was created by Congress in an effort to protect children frompornography on the Internet in libraries?

(a) Virtual Child PornographyProtection Act

(b) Kid's Data Act

(c) Child Online Protection Act

(d) Communications Privacy Act

Answer: (c)

46. Which of the following is one of the conditions that must bemet for information to be considered obscene?

(a) The information must bewitnessed by a reasonable size audience

(b) The information must be deemed obscene by a reasonableperson

(c) The work, taken as a whole,lacks serious literary, artistic, political, or scientific value

(d) There is a significant interestin sex that would offend a reasonable person

Answer: (b)

47. The textbook defines howmany types of adultery?

(a) 1

(b) 2

(c) 3

(d) 4

Answer: (a)

48. Some modern statutes usewhich term rather than theterm vagrancy?

(a) Loitering

(b) Pandering

(c) Panhandling

(d) Trafficking

Answer: (a)

49. In 2015, surveys indicated thathomelessness in the Los Angeles area of California had jumped during the previous two years.

(a) 8%

(b) 12%

(c) 16%

(d) 20%

Answer: (b)

50. Which of the following is not one of the terms mentioned inthe text that have been used to describe a variety of behaviors that some people find offensive to the extent that the criminal law is invoked to try to curb them?

(a) Lewd

(b) Lascivious

(c) Lecherous

(d) Sexual

Answer: (d)

51. Which circuit is called asregenerative repeaters?

(a) Analog circuits

(b) Digital circuits

(c) Amplifiers

(d) A/D converters

Answer: b

Explanation: The main advantage ofdigital communication is that the signals can be reproduced easily. Thus digital circuits are called asregenerative repeaters.

52. What are the advantages ofdigital circuits?

(a) Less noise
(b) Less interference
(c) More flexible
(d) All of the mentioned
Answer: d
Explanation: Digital circuits are lesssubject to noise, distortion and interference as it works on digital pulses and also the pulses can be regenerated.

53. How many different combinations can be made from a nbit value?
(a) 2(n+1)
(b) 2(n)
(c) 2(n)+1
(d) None of the mentioned
Answer: b
Explanation: $2^{(n)}$ different combinations can be made from nbit value. For example, from 2 bit value 2^2 different combinations- 00,01,10,11 can be made.

54. How many bytes does a gigabytehave?
(a) 1 million bytes
(b) 10 million bytes
(c) 1 billion bytes
(d) 10 billion bytes
Answer: c
Explanation: One gigabyte has 1billion bytes.

55. What is the ASCII value of space?
(a) 32
(b) 48
(c) 96
(d) 65
Answer: a
Explanation: The ASCII value of space is 32 and ASCII value of 0 is 48.

56. Which block or device does thedata compression?
(a) Channel encoder
(b) Source encoder
(c) Modulator
(d) None of the mentioned
Answer: b
Explanation: Source encoder converts the digital or analog signalto a sequence of binary digits. This process is called as source encodingor compression.

57. What is the code rate?
(a) k/n
(b) n/k
(c) All of the mentioned
(d) None of the mentioned
Answer: a
Explanation: Here n is the total bits of sequence and k bits are mapped. Amount of redundancy introduced isgiven by n/k and its reciprocal is the code rate.

58. Pulse shaping is done by whichblock or system?
(a) Encoder
(b) Baseband modulator
(c) Pulse code modulator
(d) Demodulator
Answer: c
Explanation: Pulse code modulator does filtering process to build pulsesthat occupy more than one bit time.

59. Equalizer is used for?

(a) Filtering

(b) Diminish distortion

(c) All of the mentioned

(d) None of the mentioned

Answer: c

Explanation: Equalizer is used as a filtering option and also diminishesor reduces the distortion.

60. Source coding block is used for?

(a) Compressing

(b) Digitizing

(c) A/D conversion

(d) All of the mentioned

Answer: d

Explanation: Source encoding doesall these processes-compression, digitizing the signal and performs analog to digital conversion.

61. Which measurement considersphase as an important parameter?

(a) Coherent

(b) Non-coherent

(c) All of the mentioned

(d) None of the mentioned

Answer: a

Explanation: Coherent measurementconsiders phase as an important parameter.

62. The size of the alphabet M insymbol is calculated as?

(a) a) 2(k+1)

(b) b) 2k

(c) c) 2(k-1)

(d) d) 1+2k

Answer: b

Explanation: The size of the alphabetis calculated using 2^k where k is thenumber of bits in the symbol.

63. Which of the followingstatements is correct?

(a) Health promotion can refer to any event, process or activity that facilitates the protection or improvement of the health status of individuals, groups, communities or populations.

(b) The objective of health promotion is to prolong life and to improve quality of life.

(c) Health promotion practice is often shaped by how health is conceptualized.

(d) all of these

Answer: D

64. Which of the following chartersdefined health promotion as 'the process of enabling people to increase control over, and to improve, their health'.

(a) Charter of the United Nations (1945)

(b) Tokyo Charter (1946)

(c) Ottawa Charter (1986)

(d) none of these

Answer: C

65. This approach to health promotion is based on the assumption that humans are rationaldecision-makers, this approach reliesheavily upon the provision of information about risks and benefitsof certain behaviours.

(a) behaviour change approach

(b) community development approach

(c) biomedical approach

(d) none of these

Answer: A

66. This approach to health promotion aims to improve and promote health by addressing socioeconomic and environmental determinants of health within thecommunity.

(a) behaviour change approach
(b) community development approach
(c) biomedical approach
(d) none of these
Answer: B

67. This approach to health promotion is synonymous with health education as it aims to increase individuals' knowledge about the causes of health andillness.
(a) behaviour change approach
(b) community development approach
(c) biomedical approach
(d) none of these
Answer: A

68. A systematic review of fear appeal research by Ruiter, Kessels,Peters and Kok (2014) concluded that______.
(a) fear tactics are the most appropriate strategy to promote healthy behaviour
(b) presenting coping information that increases perceptions of response effectiveness may be more effective in promoting healthy behaviour than presenting fear arousing stimuli
(c) no conclusions can be made concerning the effectiveness of fear tactics in promoting healthy behaviour
(d) none of these
Answer: B

69. ______refers to the applicationof consumer-oriented marketing techniques in the design, implementation and evaluation ofprogrammes aimed towards influencing behaviour change.
(a) Health education
(b) Social marketing
(c) Consumer health
(d) none of these
Answer: B

70. Which of the following is a criticism of the behaviour changeapproach to health promotion?
(a) It is unable to target the major causes of ill health.
(b) The choice of which behaviour to target lies with 'experts' whose task it is to communicate and justify this choice to the public.
(c) The behaviour change paradigm does not address the many variables other than cognitions that influence human actions.
(d) all of these
Answer: D

71. Which of the following is a characteristic of the community development approach to healthpromotion?
(a) Improving individual attitudes and beliefs are key to successful health promotion.
(b) There is a close relationship between individual health and its social and material contexts, thus are relevant when developing initiatives for change.
(c) Individuals need to change personal behaviour rather than to change the environment to promote health.
(d) all of these
Answer: B

72. Which of the following approaches to community psychology aim to connect intra-community processes with the broader socio-political context?
(a) behaviourist approach
(b) accomodationist approach
(c) critical approach
(d) none of these
Answer: C

73. Who is the author of 'Unto ThisLast'?
(a) John Ruskin
(b) Ruskin Bond
(c) Hermann Kallenbach
(d) Louis Fischer

Ans: A

74. Which of the following, according to Gandhiji, is an essentialprinciple of Satyagraha?
(a) Infinite capacity for suffering
(b) Non violence
(c) Truth
(d) All the three
Ans: D
Explanation: 'Satyagraha' is the mostimportant weapon of Gandhi ji. It emerged as a weapon of conflict resolution. Gandhi ji applied satyagraha in the non-violent struggle against exploitation, injustice and dictatorship.

75. Gandhiji's "The Story of My Experiments with Truth" was originally written in Gujarati. Whotranslated it into English?
(a) Maganlal Gandhi
(b) Mahadev Desai
(c) Pyarelalji
(d) Sushila Nayyar
Ans: B
Explanation: Mahadev Desai was anactivist of Indian freedom movement. He is best known for his job of Mahatma Gandhi's personalsecretary. He died on 15 August 1942.

76. Which one of the followingbooks is the work of Gandhiji?
(a) Light of India
(b) Hind Swaraj
(c) My Experiments with Truth
(d) Both B & C
Ans: D
Explanation: The Story of My Experiments with Truth is an autobiography of Gandhi ji. This book covers life of Gandhi ji from early childhood through to 1921. It was published in his journal Navjivanfrom 1925 to 1929.

77. When Ganadhi ji won Nobelpeace Prize?
(a) A. 1937
(b) B. 1947
(c) C. 1939
(d) D. Never
Ans: D
Explanation: Gandhi Ji never won Nobel peace Prize although Gandhi was nominated in 1937, 1938, 1939,1947 and, finally, a few days beforehe was murdered in January 1948.

78. Who established the Natal IndianCongress (NIC)?
(a) Vallabhbhai Patel
(b) Sarojini Naidu
(c) Jawaharlal Nehru
(d) None of the above
Ans: D
Explanation: On 22 May, 1894 Gandhi established the Natal Indian Congress (NIC) and worked hard to improve rights of Indians inSouth Africa.

79. When Gandhi ji returned toIndia from South Africa?
(a) A. 1918
(b) B. 1910
(c) C. 1915
(d) D. 1905
Ans: C
Explanation: Gandhi ji returned to India in 1915 permanently and joined the Indian National Congresswith Gopal Krishna Gokhale as his mentor.

80. Book 'The Satyahrah' was originally written in ....
(a) English
(b) Hindi

(c) Gujarati
(d) Bengali
Ans: C

81. Who was the political Guru ofMahatma Gandhi ji?
(a) Gopal Krishna Gokhale
(b) Dayanand Saraswati
(c) Ravindra Nath Tagore
(d) None of the above
Ans: A
Explanation: Mahatma Gandhi usedto seek the opinion of the Gopal Krishna Gokhale through letters from South Africa. Gokhale was the one who persuaded Gandhi to cameback to India, invest time in understanding India and work for Indian independence struggle movement.

82. What was the name of mother ofMahatma Gandhi?
(a) Leelawati
(b) Putlibai
(c) Sharda Bai
(d) Kusuma Devi
Answer: B
Explanation: Father of Mahatma Gandhi was Karamchand Uttamchand Gandhi while mother'sname was Putlibai Gandhi.

83. Marginalisation means :-
(a) At the centre of thing
(b) Forced to occupy the side
(c) Both (a) & (b)
(d) None of these
Ans : (b)

84. In social environment, Marginalisation is due to :-
(a) Different Language
(b) Different Religion
(c) Minority
(d) All of these
Ans : (d)

85. Explain the reason why groupsmay be marginalized.
(a) Because of government profit
(b) Less Majority
(c) Both (a) & (b)
(d) All of these
Ans : (c)

86. Who are Adivasi?
(a) Original Inhabitants
(b) tribals
(c) Both (a) & (b)
(d) None of these
Ans : (c)

87. How many percent of India'spopulation is Adivasi?
(a) Around 8%
(b) about 10%
(c) About 4%
(d) about 6%
Ans : (a)

88. Scheduled Tribes is term used for :-
(a) Rich people

(b) Adivasis
(c) People below poverty line
(d) All of these
Ans : (b)

89. Adivasi are involved in theworship of :-
(a) Ancestors
(b) Hinduism
(c) jesus Chirst
(d) temple
Ans : (a)

90. The village spirits areworshipped at :-
(a) home
(b) Town
(c) Specific Scared Groves
(d) All of these
Ans : (c)

91. Do Adivasi live close to theforest?
(a) No
(b) May be
(c) Yes
(d) Can't say
Ans : (c)

92. Adivasi languages have often deeply influenced by the formation of:-
(a) Mainstream
(b) Bengali
(c) Sanskrit
(d) Santhali
Ans : (a)

93. Adivasis are believed to be :-
(a) Exotic
(b) Primitive
(c) Backward
(d) All of these
Ans : (d)

94. Where all the important metalsare present in India?
(a) Forest
(b) Village
(c) Home
(d) Jungle
Ans : (a)

95. 1835 onwards, Adivasis from Jharkhand & adjoining areas movedin India & the world's like :-
(a) Mauritius
(b) Caribbean
(c) Australia
(d) All of these
Ans : (d)

96. Niyamgiri hill located inKalahandi district of :-
(a) Orissa
(b) West Bengal
(c) Punjab
(d) kerela

Ans : (a)

97. Niyamgiri is a scared mountain of :-
(a) Adivasis
(b) Religious people
(c) Both (a) & (b)
(d) None of these
Ans : (a)

98. How many national parks arethere in India?
(a) 64
(b) 54
(c) 72
(d) 82
Ans : (b)

99. How many wild life sanctuariescovering 1,09,652 square kilometer :-
(a) 570
(b) 458
(c) 372
(d) 190
Ans : (c)

100. The areas where tribal originallylived and continue to stay in these fields :-
(a) Ancestors
(b) Encroachers
(c) Both (a) & (b)
(d) All of these
Ans : (b)

101. Constitution provides safeguards to religious & ___________ minorities as a part of fundamental Rights.
(a) Linguistic
(b) Cultural
(c) Both (a) & (b)
(d) None of these
Ans : (c)

102. Minority means :-
(a) Used for the communities that isnumerically small in population
(b) Used for the communities that isnumerically small in population
(c) More groups
(d) All of these
Ans : (b)

103. Many tribal children are ______.
(a) Balanced
(b) Malnourished
(c) Healthy
(d) Efficient
Ans : (b)

104. Why do we need safeguards?
(a) To protect the state
(b) To protect the society
(c) To protect the rich people
(d) To protect minority community
Ans : (d)

105. Who plays a crucial role inupholding the law enforcing fundamental Rights?

(a) Judiciary
(b) Supreme Court
(c) High Court
(d) All of these
Ans : (b)

106. Every citizen of India can approach the courts if they believethat their fundamental Rights havebeen :-
(a) Increased
(b) Decreased
(c) Violating
(d) None of these
Ans : (c)

107. How many percent of Muslimsare in Indian population?
(a) 13.4%
(b) 61%
(c) 14.7%
(d) 20%
Ans : (a)

108. How many Muslims live in kutcha house according to amenties1994
(a) a. 63.6%
(b) b. 43%
(c) c. 67%
(d) d. 87%
Ans : (a)

109. Do Muslims have equal accessto basic amenities?
(a) yes
(b) may be
(c) No
(d) Can't not
Ans : (c)

110. According to literacy rate by religion, 2001 how many percent ofpopulation is literate?
(a) 65%
(b) 100%
(c) 95%
(d) 80%
Ans : (a)

111. Which religious group has thelowest literacy rate according to censes of India 2001?
(a) Hindus
(b) Muslims
(c) Sikh
(d) English
Ans : (b)

112. High level committee in 2005,was chaired by :-
(a) Hakkim shekh
(b) Ram Gopal
(c) Rajinder Sanchar
(d) None of these
Ans : (c)

113. Many Muslim women wear?
(a) Burka
(b) Skirt
(c) Payjama

(d) Cargo
Ans : (a)

114. Marginalisation is linked to :-
 (a) Experiencing disadvantages
 (b) Prejudices
 (c) Powerless
 (d) All of these
Ans : (d)

115. Marginalisation result in having :-
(a) Low social status
(b) Not equal education
(c) Both (a) & (b)
(d) None of these
Ans : (c)

116. Muslims prefer to send theirchildren to :-
(a) Madarsas
(b) Schools
(c) Colleges
(d) All of these
Ans : (a)

117. Hierarchy means :-
(a) A graded system or arrangement of person or thing
(b) Minor group
(c) Major group
(d) None of these
Ans : (a)

118. Displaced means :-
(a) To stick at one place
(b) to live in forest
(c) Refuse to forced or compelled tomove from their homes
(d) All of these
Ans : (c)

119. Militarised means :-
(a) Presence of Minor Group
(b) Presence of Major group
(c) Presence of Adivasis
(d) presence of armed force
Ans : (d)

120. Malnourishment means :-
(a) Person gets a balance diet
(b) Person gets the extra diet
(c) Person does not get adequatefood
(d) None of these
Ans : (c)

121. Which one of the following ismain cause of Marginalisation?
(a) Different dress
(b) Different films
(c) Different Languages
(d) All of these
Ans : (c)

122. Marginalised groups are viewedwith hostility.

(a) respect

(b) truth

(c) Fear

(d) All of these

Ans : (c)

123. Give another name of Adivasis

(a) Respective truth

(b) Tribals

(c) Educated person

(d) None of these

Ans : (b)

124. Is Adivasis having their ownlanguage?

(a) No

(b) Can't say

(c) May be

(d) Yes

Ans : (d)

125. Which one of the followingmetal is found in forest?

(a) Sugar

(b) Sweet

(c) Iron

(d) Tea

Ans : (c)

126. Literacy rate among tribal arevery______

(a) High

(b) Low

(c) In between

(d) Supreme

Ans : (c)

127._are needed toprotect minor Communities.

(a) Safeguards

(b) Legal

(c) Laws

(d) None of these

Ans : (b)

128. How many percent of Muslimsare in India's population?

(a) 1.34%

(b) 22.3%

(c) 15.1%

(d) 20.0%

Ans : (a)

129._are the importantpart of the women's movement in India?

(a) Religious Women

(b) Common people

(c) Muslim women

(d) None of these

Ans : (c)

130. Marginalisation results in :-

(a) Low social status

(b) not equal access of Eduation

(c) Both (a) & (b)

(d) None of these

Ans : (c)

131. How many percent of Muslimchildren in the 6 - 14 year of age group have never been enrolled inschools & dropped out?

(a) a. 70%

(b) b. 30%

(c) c. 25%

(d) d. 56%

Ans : (c)

132. In Muslim community, there is alink between economic &___marginalisation.

(a) Political

(b) western

(c) Socio reform

(d) Social

Ans : (d)

133. Richard Shwederdefines 'cultural collisions' as:

(a) when cultural artifacts are combined

(b) situations where different cultural groups come into contact

(c) urban planning that takes into account ethnic heritage

(d) when individuals from different ethnic heritages disagree

Answer: B

134. Which of the following IS NOT trueabout female genital surgery?

(a) procedures may involve mild or severe modifications to the genital region

(b) this practice connects to cultural identity

(c) worldwide this practice is most prevalent in Australia

(d) one cultural reason for the practice is cultural standards of beauty

Answer: C

135. Richard Shweder argues there is a double standard with respect to female genital surgery. Whichstatement best supports his argument?

(a) the practice exists in part because of cultural norms and values

(b) the procedure is acceptable for a Western woman who elects the procedure but barbaric for an African woman who desires the procedure

(c) this is a procedure that is a cultural collision

(d) outsiders are accepting of the procedure

Answer: B

136. An attitude is:

(a) our reaction to events and experiences in our environment that shape our actions

(b) our reaction to events that create emotions responses

(c) a perspective present at birth

(d) a perspective or belief that is not culture-specific

Answer: A

137. Which of the followingis an example of an attitude?

(a) I really like your shirt.

(b) Our family has a new pet.

(c) I am interested in studying cultural psychology.

(d) I am thinking of a career in medicine.

Answer: A

138. Prejudice is:

(a) our reaction to events and experiences in our environment that shape our actions

(b) our reaction to events that create emotional responses

(c) a perspective present at birth

(d) a learned attitude that shapes the way we think and act toward other people and social groups

Answer: D

139. Which of the followingis an example of prejudice?

(a) only girls should play with dolls
(b) I would not hire any person under the age of 30 for this position
(c) I like Portuguese food
(d) I don't like old folks
Answer: D

140. Which of the following IS NOT acomponent of attitudes?

(a) cognitive
(b) affective
(c) personal
(d) behavioral
Answer: C

141. A stereotype is:

(a) a belief assigned to an entire group
(b) present at birth
(c) our actions towards entire groups
(d) a perceived threat due to cultural differences in beliefs
Answer: A

142. Which of the following IS NOT a function of stereotypes?

(a) they help us describe in-groups
(b) they help us describe out-groups
(c) they help us validate our in-group and undervalue out-groups
(d) connect to how we think about people and social groups
Answer: A

143. Which of the followingis an example of a stereotype?

(a) a perceived threat due to contact with an out-group member
(b) anxiety due to contact with a stranger
(c) only women make good nurses
(d) your negative treatment of an out-group member
Answer: C

144. Discrimination is:

(a) a belief assigned to an entire group
(b) present at birth
(c) our actions towards entire groups
(d) a perceived threat due to cultural differences in beliefs
Answer: C

145. Discrimination differsfrom prejudice and stereotypes becausediscrimination:

(a) involves our actions and the way we treat others because of their group membership
(b) is a learned attitude
(c) is a belief system present at birth
(d) never has negative or damaging consequences
Answer: A

146. One important difference betweendiscrimination, prejudice, and stereotypes is that discrimination:

(a) involves our beliefs about others because of their group membership
(b) is a learned attitude
(c) is a belief system present at birth
(d) has an emotional component
Answer: D

147. Which of the followingis an example of discrimination?

(a) Younger workers are not loyal to their companies
(b) I would never want to work for a woman.
(c) Asian children are high achievers
(d) I hate customer service representatives who aren't helpful
Answer: D

148. In their work on stereotypes, Cuddy,Norton, and Fiske found:

(a) most participants viewed the elderly both positively and negatively

(b) participants in communities that emphasize a respect for elders held different views than other participants
(c) one explanation for participant responses is social media
(d) no ageism emerged in their study
Answer: A

149. Inter-group anxietyrefers to:
(a) unfavorable perceptions we hold about out-group individuals
(b) threats we experience due to our experiences
(c) anxiety from real or anticipated contact with an out-group individual
(d) perceived threats due to cultural differences in beliefs and practices
Answer: C

150. Negative stereotypesare:
(a) unfavorable perceptions we hold about out-group individuals
(b) threats we experience due to our experiences
(c) anxiety from real or anticipated contact with an out-group individual
(d) perceived threats due to cultural differences in beliefs and practices
Answer: A

151. Realistic threats are:
(a) unfavorable perceptions we hold about out-group individuals
(b) threats we experience due to actual experiences with our-group members
(c) anxiety from real or anticipated contact with an out-group individual
(d) perceived threats due to cultural differences in beliefs and practices
Answer: B

152. Symbolic threats are:
(a) unfavorable perceptions we hold about out-group individuals
(b) threats we experience due to our experiences
(c) anxiety from real or anticipated contact with an out-group individual
(d) perceived threats due to cultural differences in beliefs and practices
Answer: D

153. In their study with Dutch workers, Curseuand colleagues found:
(a) symbolic threats were more influential in determining ethnic prejudice toward immigrants
(b) realistic threats were more influential in determining ethnic prejudice toward immigrants
(c) negative stereotypes were more influential in determining ethnic prejudice toward immigrants
(d) inter-group anxiety was more influential in determining ethnic prejudice toward immigrants
Answer: C

154. In their study with Dutch workers, Curseuand colleagues found that:
(a) repeated positive interactions with immigrants reduced all threats and negative stereotypes
(b) repeated positive interactions with immigrants reduced negative stereotypes
(c) repeated positive interactions with immigrants reduced all threats
(d) repeated positive interactions had no impact on Dutch worker and immigrant relationships
Answer: A

155. The Stereotype Content Model is useful for studies on:
(a) symbolic threats
(b) inter-group anxiety
(c) realistic threats
(d) stereotypes
Answer: D

156. The Stereotype Content Model uses two traits to study stereotypes. They are:
(a) warmth and competence
(b) warmth and nurturance
(c) warmth and power
(d) status and power
Answer: A

157. You are interested in studying stereotypes. Which of the followingrelates to the dimension warmth in the Stereotype Content Model?

(a) a group's ability to work cooperatively
(b) social status
(c) power
(d) positive attitudes
Answer: A

158. Glick and colleagues studied college students worldwide regarding their perceptions of the USand its citizens after the 9/11 attack. Theyfound:
(a) US citizens were competent, arrogant, and cold
(b) the US government was more arrogant than its citizens
(c) the US government showed more concern for cooperating with other nations
(d) the US government showed no desire to exploit others
Answer: B

159. Which of the following IS NOT trueabout colorism?
(a) it is the biased treatment of individuals based upon skin color
(b) it is a type of prejudice
(c) it is a type of discrimination
(d) it appears in every cultural community worldwide
Answer: D

160. Evidence suggests thata preference for fair skin in India connects to all of the following EXCEPT:
(a) Hinduism
(b) British colonization
(c) the caste system
(d) modernization
Answer: D

161. The origins of light skinpreference in the US connect to which of the following?
(a) slavery
(b) the Civil Rights Act
(c) interethnic romantic unions
(d) social media
Answer: A

162. Implicit bias is:
(a) an unintentional and unconscious bias towards light-skinned individuals
(b) a learned attitude
(c) a stereotype
(d) a bias on the basis of social status
Answer: A

163. In a study that explored cultural mismatch between jurors and defendants,the authors found thatEuropean American jurors were more likelyto render a guilty verdict when the defendant was dark- skinned. This is an example of:
(a) a stereotype
(b) implicit bias
(c) a learned attitude
(d) discrimination
Answer: B

164. What is one possibleexplanation for skin color bias in Mexico?
(a) slavery
(b) a person's occupation
(c) Spanish colonization
(d) implicit bias
Answer: C

165. Xenophobia is:
(a) an irrational fear of heights
(b) an irrational fear of water
(c) an irrational fear of the unfamiliar
(d) an irrational fear of snakes
Answer: C

166. One explanation for the hostility some people feel towards immigrants is:

(a) implicit bias
(b) prejudice
(c) stereotype
(d) xenophobia
Answer: D

167. Yakushko suggests that hostility towards immigrants is due to all the following EXCEPT:

(a) xenophobia
(b) ethnocentrism
(c) economic struggles
(d) implicit bias
Answer: D

168. Out-group entitativity describes:

(a) how outsiders perceive a group's strength to act together to achieve shared goals
(b) negative perceptions of an out- group
(c) an unconscious bias toward light- skinned individuals
(d) an irrational fear of the unfamiliar
Answer: A

169. In their work with Norwegian college students, Ommundsen and colleagues found that:

(a) native born Norwegians did not perceive Muslims as a cohesive group
(b) positive interactions increased fears of xenophobia
(c) when native born Norwegians perceived Muslims as a cohesive group, fears of xenophobia increased
(d) when native born Norwegians perceived Muslims as a cohesive group, fears of xenophobia decreased
Answer: C

170. Which of the following IS NOT a strategy some immigrants may use to adjust to their new home?

(a) they maintain their cultural traditions
(b) they maintain their cultural values
(c) they seek out members of their in- group for a sense of belonging
(d) they assimilate to the host country as soon as possible
Answer: D

171. Which of the following is the cause of much psychological distress for immigrants and their children?

(a) learning a new language
(b) finding a job
(c) pressure to assimilate
(d) finding a place to live
Answer: C

172. Acculturation is:

(a) a type of implicit bias
(b) an adjustment process that most immigrants experience
(c) a type of stereotype
(d) a form of xenophobia
Answer: B

173. Berry introduced several different orientations that help immigrants adjust to their new community. They include all of the following EXCEPT:

(a) assimilation
(b) integration
(c) separation
(d) enculturation
Answer: D

174. A Liberian family now living in Austria has adopted its new country's values while retaining their native Liberian cultural values. According to Berry, this is an example of which orientation:

(a) assimilation
(b) integration
(c) separation
(d) marginalization
Answer: B

175. A Uruguayan family that moved to Costa Rica decides to highly value Uruguayan values and traditions while also choosing to isolate themselves from the dominant majority in their new home. According to Berry, this is an example of which orientation:

(a) assimilation
(b) integration
(c) separation
(d) marginalization
Answer: C

176. Integrated threat theory explains:

(a) stereotypes between different social groups
(b) implicit bias between different social groups
(c) inter-anxiety between different social groups
(d) the causes of threats between different social groups
Answer: D

177. Many immigrants experience a loss of their cultural identity when moving to a new country. The term for this experience is:

(a) implicit bias
(b) identity theft
(c) xenophobia
(d) separation
Answer: B

178. Which strategy might an immigrant family use to reduce the stress of coming into contact and interacting with members of their new host country?

(a) xenophobia
(b) identity theft
(c) implicit bias
(d) cultural retention
Answer: D

179. Biculturalism is all of the following EXCEPT:

(a) a good strategy to help immigrants adjust to their new home
(b) the ability to interact in more than one cultural setting
(c) the ability to speak more than one language
(d) something many teenage immigrant children experience in adjusting to their new home
Answer: C

180. Schwebel and Hodari's case study of a Filipino teenage boy adjusting to life in the US, supports the benefits of which of Berry's orientation types?

(a) integration
(b) marginalization
(c) separation
(d) assimilation
Answer: A

181. Integration as an orientation strategy for immigrants connects to which of the following?

(a) implicit bias
(b) xenophobia
(c) biculturalism
(d) cultural retention
Answer: C

182. The contact hypothesis predicts that when in- group and out-group members have face to face interactions and share cooperative goals these should:

(a) increase intergroup anxiety and stereotypical thinking
(b) decrease symbolic threats and stereotypical thinking
(c) decrease prejudice, discrimination, and stereotypical thinking
(d) increase prejudice, discrimination, and stereotypical thinking
Answer: C

183. The contact hypothesishelps reduce:

(a) stereotypes
(b) implicit bias
(c) assimilation
(d) acculturation
Answer: A

184.A longitudinalapproach:

(a) is a short term research design
(b) a research design that lasts for an extended period
(c) must take place in only one cultural setting
(d) must take place in numerous cultural settings
Answer: B

185. Binder and colleagues studied ethnic majorityand minority children in Germany to learn about intergroup contact and prejudice. Which of the followingdid their findings support?

(a) the contact hypothesis
(b) implicit bias
(c) xenophobia
(d) acculturation
Answer: A

186. Which cultural creation was a symbol of a cultural collision inAustralia and France?

(a) the canoe
(b) the burkini
(c) female genital surgery
(d) sculptures made of paper
Answer: B

187. In their work with Portuguese children ofEuropean (majority) and African (minority) ethnic heritages, Guerra and colleaguesfound that:

(a) children who kept their ethnic identity had more positive views of out-group members
(b) children from the minority ethnic group preferred their ethnic identity label over a shared identity label
(c) children who shared a common group identity label had more positive views of out-group members
(d) children from the majority ethnic group preferred a shared group identity label over their ethnic identity label
Answer: C

188. Who is more likely toexperience skill discounting?

(a) a native born Canadian applying for a managerial position in Canada
(b) a native born Australian applying for an hospital internship in Australia
(c) a Peruvian doctor applying for a medical residency in the US
(d) a native born Columbian applying for a teaching position in Columbia
Answer: C

189. In their study on skill discounting among adult Canadians, Essesand colleagues found that several factors influenced applicant evaluation in their hypothetical hiring scenario. This includedall the following EXCEPT:

(a) where the applicant received training
(b) the applicant's birthplace
(c) attitudes towards immigrants
(d) implicit bias
Answer: D

190. What is one stereotypethat many Western educators have of Asian children?

(a) they actively engage in class discussions
(b) they are quiet and passive at school
(c) they are high achievers in language arts
(d) they are extroverted in all social contexts
Answer: B

191. In the Chinese worldview, knowing when to be quiet is a positive skill because:

(a) children defer to authority
(b) being quiet indicates concentration
(c) being quiet indicates children have learned to accommodate their behavior to specific social contexts

(d) it indicates that children are striving for uniqueness

Answer: C

192. What cultural values shape many Chinese children's decision notto directly confront or challenge a teacher inclass?

(a) modesty and group cohesion
(b) self-expression
(c) assertiveness
(d) uniqueness

Answer: A

193. In their study that explored how cultural norms and practices shape perceptions of quietness among Chinese parents and teachers, Yamamoto and Li compared the perceptions of Chineseimmigrant and native born European American children attending schools that had both Asian teachers and EuropeanAmerican teachers. They found that:

(a) Asian teachers evaluated quietness as a positive quality that connected to learning
(b) teachers rated Chinese immigrant children as quieter only in the Asian contexts
(c) teachers correlated quietness for Chinese immigrant children who attended European American schools with student learning
(d) there was no cultural mismatch in perceptions between either group of teachers

Answer: A

194. Social justice is a construct in which:

(a) no individual should receive equal treatment and access to resources in any society
(b) no individual should receive equal care and power in a society
(c) no individual should receive equal treatment, care, and access to resources in a society
(d) all individuals should receive equal treatment, care, and access to resources and power in a society

Answer: D

195. Which of the followingis not an overriding theme and social justice?

(a) fairness
(b) access
(c) opportunity
(d) individual wealth

Answer: D

196. Which of the following IS NOT a difficulty some Moroccan immigrantsare experiencing in their new home, Spain?

(a) acquiring good jobs
(b) language barriers
(c) an inability to travel to receive services
(d) living in affluent neighborhoods

Answer: D

197. According to Paloma and colleagues, what isone way to help ensure social justice?

(a) access to community services
(b) access to good paying jobs
(c) learning the language
(d) assimilating to their new home's cultural values, beliefs, and practices

Answer: A

198. What is a distinguishing factor ofTibetan immigrants?

(a) they demonstrate a personal and cultural connection and concern for social justice in their native homeland and new home
(b) they are subject to oppression and discrimination more than any other ethnic group
(c) they never received the support of social service agencies
(d) when living under Chinese rule they experienced little oppression

Answer: A

199. The meaning of the gesture 'thumbs up' isculture specific. Whatdoes the gesture 'thumbs up' mean inNigeria?

(a) all is well
(b) I'm okay
(c) it is a rude gesture
(d) I'm very happy

Answer: C

200. The bow in many countries and culturalcommunities that practice this custom and gesture is a sign of:

(a) respect
(b) humility
(c) submission
(d) a simple greeting
Answer: A

201. Recent immigrants, students studying abroad, and fieldworkers engagingin fieldwork in foreignregions are all likely to experience:

(a) implicit bias
(b) culture shock
(c) cultural relativism
(d) assimilation
Answer: B

202. Intercultural competence is:

(a) the ability to communicate with people from different cultural communities
(b) the ability to adjust to a new cultural setting
(c) learning cultural practices very quickly
(d) being sensitive to new cultural customs and practices
Answer: A

203. Which of the followingwould reflect prevailing ideas in comparative social science about the nature of race?

(a) Race is fundamentally a matter of biology.
(b) Racial categories as such appear to be socially or culturally constructed.
(c) Since race is not really biological, it does not have political consequences.
(d) We live in a "post-racial" world.
Answer: B

204. Which of the followingstatements about gender would be judged least plausible by the social-scientific community?

(a) Gender is receiving greater attention from scholars in comparative politics than in the past.
(b) Gender and biological sex mean the same thing.
(c) Gender is more cultural whereas sex is more biological.
(d) Gender remains an important factor in politics.
Answer: B

205. Which of the followingclaims is not true, according to social scientists?

(a) Gender and ethnicity are both constructed categories.
(b) Gender and ethnicity intersect with political party formation in precisely the same way.
(c) One way to try to empower members of disadvantaged groups is through institutional design strategies like quota systems and reserved seats.
(d) Gender and ethnicity have a complicated and varying relationship with the major strategies used to empower members of diverse groups.
Answer: B

206. Why do social scientists believe that, even after modern progress, discrimination on the basis of race, ethnicity,and gender persists?

(a) Evidence from methods like audit studies reveal ongoing discrimination.
(b) Different groups have measurable differences in various socioeconomic outcomes.
(c) A number of members of disadvantaged groups report experiencing discrimination.
(d) All of the above
Answer: D

207. Which of the followingis a type of gender empowerment discussed in this chapter?

(a) Self-esteem empowerment
(b) Political empowerment
(c) Biological empowerment
(d) Sociological empowerment
Answer: B

208. What is the core explanation that MalaHtun gives for the factthat gender-based parties are less common than ethnic parties?

(a) Ethnic categories cut across other categories that serve as the basis for party formation.

(b) Gender categories cut across other categories that serve as the basis for party formation.
(c) Ethnic groups are simply more culturally disposed to form parties.
(d) Patriarchy
Answer: B

209. Which of the followingideas is one of the factors cited in Donna Lee Van Cott's argument about the creation of ethnic parties in Latin America?
(a) Ethnic parties emerged because of charismatic leaders.
(b) Ethnic parties emerged in part because archaeological evidence made people realize who they "really are."
(c) Ethnic parties emerged in part because decentralization created new political opportunities while old bases of mobilization for marginalized groups were weakened.
(d) Ethnic parties emerged because of dependent economic development.
Answer: C

210. Which of the following factors plays a prominent role in Joanne Nagel's accountof the dramatic growthof the share of the U.S.population self- identifying as "NativeAmerican" or "American Indian" inthe mid- to late twentieth century?
(a) Independent monitoring by the EU
(b) "Red Power" Activism
(c) The decline of the Democratic Party
(d) The decline of the Republican party
Answer: B

211. Which sorts of actors,among others, does Mona Lena Krook's argument lead us to expect to play an important role in determining whethergender quotas will be
adopted in a givenpolity?
(a) Rural laborers, religious leaders, and the media
(b) Politicians acting strategically, transnational organizations, and activists
(c) Economic classes, trade unions, and the bourgeoisie
(d) None of the above
Answer: B

212. Which of the followingis frequently cited by comparative politics scholars to influence the likelihood of the formation of ethnic parties?
(a) Judicial review
(b) Terrorism
(c) Existing interest groups and sources of political cleavage in the society in question
(d) None of the above
Answer: C

213. Why do some scholarsin comparative politicsthink that political empowerment might
lead to other forms ofempowerment?
(a) All of economics and culture is based on politics.
(b) You can have an effect on economics only if you have political power.
(c) You can only impact culture if you have political power.
(d) Some research shows that women who hold office are, on average, more inclined than male office-holders to value equity highly.
Answer: D

214. Which of the followingcountries has seen significant improvement in women's rights over the last several decades?
(a) Brazil
(b) Iran
(c) Saudi Arabia
(d) None of the above
Answer: A

215. Which of the followingis probably not a factorinfluencing the likelihood that ethnic parties will be formed?
(a) Ethnic demographics
(b) History of conflict between groups
(c) Presence or absence of other bases of cleavage
(d) Climate
Answer: D

216. Which of the followingwould not be an example of a social movement mobilizing around an ethnic identity?

(a) Iran's "Green Revolution"
(b) The French Revolution
(c) The Landless Movement in Brazil
(d) None of the above
Answer: D

217. According to the perspective of this chapter, which of the following claims is notdemonstrably true?
(a) Institutional design solutions to problems of group inequality are often effective.
(b) Social movements can be useful ways to address inequality.
(c) Social movements, political parties, and institutional design responses to group inequalities often go hand in hand.
(d) You can have social movements or parties, but you can't have both.
Answer: D

218._ is the realization of Divinity in man
(a) Psychology
(b) Science
(c) Religion
(d) Metaphysics
Answer: C

219. Rita means
(a) Legal order
(b) Moral Order
(c) Official order
(d) Cosmic Order
Answer: D

220. Which among the following isnot accepted by Karma Doctrine
(a) Karma Phala
(b) Karma Samskara
(c) Rebirth
(d) Materialism
Answer: D

221. The sum total of Papa and Punya in the life of man constitute
(a) Ignorance
(b) Desire
(c) Karma Samskara
(d) Karma neeti
Answer: C

222. The cause of Rebirth accordingto Indian Philosophy is
(a) Karmic Bondage
(b) God
(c) Knowledge
(d) Death
Answer: A

223. Which among the following isnot the cause of ignorance
(a) Liberation
(b) Bondage
(c) Rebirth
(d) Transmigration
Answer: A

224. According to Indian philosophy'Moksha' means liberation from
(a) Life
(b) Enemy
(c) Diseases
(d) Bondages
Answer: D

225. The word 'Yoga' means
(a) Union of impermanent self with permanent self

(b) Union of life with death
(c) Union of Day with night
(d) Union of body with mind
Answer: A

226. The origin of Indian philosophical thought is in
(a) Systems
(b) Vedas
(c) Ithihasas
(d) Puranas
Answer: B

227. The word 'Veda' originatedfrom the word
(a) Vayu
(b) Vyasa
(c) Vid
(d) Vip
Answer: C

228. Vedas are also called as
(a) Smriti
(b) Chinda
(c) Sruthi
(d) Pravrittis
Answer: C

229. Which among the following isnot a Veda
(a) Rig
(b) Sama
(c) Yajur
(d) Sankhya
Answer: D

230. There are Vedas
(a) 2
(b) 3
(c) 4
(d) 5
Answer: C

231. The word 'Rik' means
(a) Verse
(b) Song
(c) Prose
(d) None of the above
Answer: A

232. The word 'yajur' means
(a) Verse b
(b) Prose.
(c) Song
(d) Grammar
Answer: B

233. The word 'Sama' means
(a) Verse
(b) Prose.
(c) Song
(d) Grammer
Answer: C

234. Veda consists of _ parts.
(a) 10
(b) 12

(c) 4
(d) 6
Answer: C

235. The part which consists ofhymns is called
(a) Mantra
(b) Brahmana
(c) Aranyaka
(d) Upanishad
Answer: A

236. The part which consists of directions for performing sacrifices iscalled
(a) Mantra
(b) Brahmana
(c) Aranyaka
(d) Upanishad
Answer: B

237. The part which consists of mystic interpretation of Brahmana iscalled
(a) Mantra
(b) Brahmana
(c) Aranyaka
(d) Upanishad
Answer: C

238. The end portion of Veda iscalled
(a) Mantra
(b) Brahmana
(c) Aranyaka
(d) Upanishad
Answer: D

239. Which one of the following isnot a Vedanga
(a) Vyakarana
(b) Jyothisha
(c) Jathaka
(d) Niruktha
Answer: C

240. The religion which believe inmany Gods is called
(a) Polytheism
(b) Henotheism
(c) Monotheism
(d) Monism
Answer: D

241.. The religion which believe inone God at a particular period is called
(a) Polytheism
(b) b, Henotheism
(c) c. Monotheism
(d) d. Monism
Answer: B

242. The religion which believe inone God is called
(a) Polytheism
(b) Henotheism
(c) Monotheism
(d) Monism
Answer: C

243. The religion which believe inone Ultimate Reality is called
(a) Polytheism
(b) Henotheism
(c) Monotheism

(d) Monism

Answer: D

244. The word 'Theism' means

(a) Belief in Caste
(b) Belief in Creed
(c) Belief in Race
(d) Belief in God

Answer: D

245. Qualified Monism mentionedabout

(a) Personalistic view of Brahman
(b) Impersonalistic view of Brahman
(c) Both
(d) None of the above

Answer: A

246. Para Brahman is

(a) Saguna Brahman
(b) Nirguna Brahman
(c) Both
(d) None

Answer: B

247. Apara Brahman is

(a) Saguna Brahman
(b) Nirguna Brahman
(c) Both
(d) None

Answer: A

248. Upanishads are also called

(a) Vedanga
(b) Vedanta
(c) Vedabhashya
(d) Vedasadana

Answer: B

249. Upanishad teaches

(a) Realism
(b) Idealistic Monism
(c) Monotheism
(d) Pragmatism

Answer: B

250. The word Brahman came fromthe word

(a) Brhanthala
(b) Brihaspati
(c) Brh
(d) Brj

Answer: C

251. According to Acosmic view

(a) Brahman alone is real
(b) The world alone is real
(c) Brahman & World are real
(d) Brahman & World are unreal

Answer: A

252. According to Cosmic view

(a) Brahman alone is real
(b) The world alone is real
(c) Brahman & World are real
(d) Brahman & World are unreal

Answer: D

253. The power of Illusion is called
(a) Brahman
(b) Maya
(c) Atman
(d) Sandhya
Answer: B

254. Who among the following is theproponent of Advaita Vedanta
(a) Sri Krishna
(b) Kanada
(c) Sri Sankaracharya
(d) Ramanuja
Answer: C

255. Who among the following is theproponent of Visishta Advaita
(a) Gautama
(b) Kanada
(c) Sri Sankaracharya
(d) Ramanuja
Answer: C

256. Individual soul is called
(a) Jivatman
(b) Paramatman
(c) Manas
(d) Indriya
Answer: A

257. Which among the following isnot a Kosa
(a) Annamaya Kosa
(b) Pranamaya Kosa
(c) Santhoshamaya Kosa
(d) Manomaya Kosa
Answer: C

258. Annamaya Kosa is called
(a) Bodly Sheath
(b) Vital Sheath
(c) Mental Sheath
(d) Intellectual Sheath
Answer: A

259. Pranamaya Kosa is called
(a) Bodly Sheath
(b) Vital Sheath
(c) Mental Sheath
(d) Intellectual Sheath
Answer: B

260. Manomaya Kosa is called
(a) Bodly Sheath
(b) Vital Sheath
(c) Mental Sheath
(d) Intellectual Sheath
Answer: C

261. Vijnanamaya Kosa is called
(a) Bodly Sheath
(b) Vital Sheath
(c) Mental Sheath
(d) Intellectual Sheath
Answer: D

262. Anandamaya Kosa is called

(a) Bodly Sheath
(b) Vital Sheath
(c) Sheath of Bliss
(d) Intellectual Sheath
Answer: C

263. First chapter of Bhagavad Gita is

(a) Samkhya Yoga
(b) Arjuna vishada Yoga
(c) Dhyana Yoga
(d) Karma Yoga
Answer: B

264. Which chapter is calledViswarupa Darsana Yoga

(a) One
(b) Thirteen
(c) Eighteen
(d) Eleven
Answer: C

265. Performing one's duties in accordance with his position in thesociety is called

(a) Nityakarma
(b) Kamyakarma
(c) Swadharma
(d) Anyadharma
Answer: C

266. Performing one's duties without any selfish motive is called

(a) Karma phala
(b) Nishkama karma
(c) Karma samskara
(d) Naimittika karma
Answer: B

267. 'Path of action in inaction' is thecontribution of

(a) Upanishads
(b) Samkhya yoga
(c) Buddhism
(d) Bhagavad Gita
Answer: B

268. Path of action towards selfrealization is called

(a) Karma marga
(b) Jnana marga
(c) Bhakti marga
(d) Raja marga
Answer: A

269. Path of wisdom towards selfrealization is called

(a) Karma marga
(b) Jnana marga
(c) Bhakti marga
(d) Raja marga
Answer: B

270. Path of devotion towards selfrealization is called

(a) Karma marga
(b) Jnana marga
(c) Bhakti marga
(d) Raja marga
Answer: C

271. Bhagavad Gita provides asynthesis of

(a) Jnana & Bhakti
(b) Jnana & karma
(c) Karma, bhakti &Jnana
(d) None of the above
Answer: C

272. Purification of mind throughNishkama karma is called

(a) Prana sudhi
(b) Chitta sudhi
(c) Tapas
(d) Dhyana
Answer: B

273.'Yoga karmasu kausalam' is theideology of

(a) Advaita Vedanta
(b) Visishta Advaita
(c) Bhagavad Gita
(d) Ramayana
Answer: C

274. The person with steady mind is called

(a) Sthitaprajna
(b) Prajna sree
(c) Vanaprastha
(d) Grahatha
Answer: A

275. Yogi satisfied with the thoughts of

(a) Self
(b) Body
(c) Sense organ
(d) Mind
Answer: A

276. The way towards self realization according to BhagavadGita is

(a) Escape from sorrow
(b) Escape from household duties
(c) Nishkama karma
(d) Swadyaya
Answer: C

277. According to Bhagavad Gita 'Preservation of world of humanity'means

(a) Sthitha prajna
(b) Environmental ethics
(c) Mukti marga
(d) Loka samgraha
Answer: D

278. Concept of 'lokasamgraha' aimsat

(a) Welfare of humanity
(b) protection of Environment
(c) Presevation of Biosphere
(d) Preservation of Nature
Answer: A

279. Social dimension of Bhakti iscalled

(a) Asrama
(b) Varna
(c) Lokasamgraha
(d) Sthithaprajna
Answer: C

280. Systems which rejected theauthority of Vedas are called

(a) a. Orthodox systems
(b) b Heterodox system
(c) c. Theism
(d) d. Atheism
Answer: B

281.Systems which accepted theauthority of Vedas are called
(a) Orthodox systems
(b) Heterodox system
(c) Theism
(d) Atheism
Answer: A

282. Orthodox systems areotherwise known as
(a) Astika darsana
(b) Nastika Darsana
(c) Theism
(d) Atheism
Answer: A

283.Heterodox systems areotherwise known as
(a) Astika darsana
(b) Nastika Darsana
(c) Theism
(d) Atheism
Answer: B

284.Which among the following isnot a Heterodox system
(a) Charvaka materialism
(b) Jainism
(c) Buddhism
(d) Purva mimamsa
Answer: D

285.Which among the following isnot a Heterodox system
(a) Charvaka materialism
(b) Advaita Vedanta
(c) Buddhism
(d) Jainism
Answer: B

286.Which among the following isnot a Heterodox system
(a) Charvaka materialism
(b) Jainism
(c) Nyaya Vaiseshika
(d) Buddhism
Answer: C

287.Which among the following isnot a Heterodox system
(a) Samkhya yoga
(b) Jainism
(c) Buddhism
(d) Charvaka materialism
Answer: A

288.Which one of the following is aHeterodox system
(a) Nyaya
(b) Buddhism
(c) Samkhya
(d) Vaiseshika
Answer: A

289.Which one of the following is aHeterodox system
(a) Jainism

(b) Yoga
(c) Purva MImamsa
(d) Vaiseshika
Answer: A

290.Which one of the following is aHeterodox system
(a) Advaita Vedanta
(b) Nyaya
(c) Charvaka Materialism
(d) Vaiseshika
Answer: C

291.Which one of the following is anOrthodox system
(a) Nyaya
(b) Jainism
(c) Buddhism
(d) Lokayata
Answer: A

292.Which among the following isnot an Orthodox system
(a) Nyaya
(b) Vaiseshika
(c) Samkhya
(d) Buddhism
Answer: D

293.Which among the following isnot an Orthodox system
(a) Charvaka Materialism
(b) Uttara Mimamsa
(c) Purva Mimamsa.
(d) Yoga
Answer: A

294.Uttara Mimamsa is otherwiseknown as
(a) Purva Mimamsa
(b) Mimamsa Sutra
(c) Advaita Vedanta
(d) Upanishad
Answer: C

295.Charvaka Materialism isotherwise known as
(a) Advaita Vedanta
(b) Lokayata
(c) Lokasamgraha
(d) Visishta Advaita
Answer: B

296.Which one of the followingelements is not accepted by Charvaka materialism
(a) Earth
(b) Air
(c) water
(d) Ether
Answer: D

297.How many pramanas are accepted by Charvaka materialism
(a) One
(b) Three
(c) Four
(d) Six
Answer: A

298.Name the Pramana accepted byLokayata
(a) Inference
(b) Comparison

(c) Perception

(d) All the above

Answer: C

299. Which among the following isaccepted by Charvaka materialism

(a) God

(b) Matter

(c) Soul

(d) Rebirth

Answer: B

300. Last chapter of Bhagavad Gita iscalled

(a) Mokshasamnyasa Yoga

(b) Samnyasa Yoga

(c) Bhakthi Yoga

(d) Vibhuti Yoga

Answer: A

301. Which among the following areParama Purusharthas according to Indian Philosophy

(a) Dharma & Moksha

(b) Artha & Kama

(c) Both a & b

(d) None of the above

Answer: C

302. Purusharthas accepted byCharvaka materialism

(a) Artha & Kama

(b) Dharma & Moksha

(c) Dharma and Kama

(d) Artha & Moksha

Answer: A

303. Which one among the followingis called 'Indian Hedonism'

(a) Buddhism

(b) Charvaka Materialism

(c) Jainism

(d) Nyaya

Answer: B

304. Who among the following is theAuthor of 'Sarva Darsana Samgraha'

(a) Gautama Buddha

(b) Pathanjali

(c) Jaimini

(d) Brihaspati

Answer: D

305. Who among the following is thefounder of Buddhism

(a) Rishabha Deva

(b) Vardhmana Mahavira

(c) Gautama Buddha

(d) Brihaspati

Answer: C

306. Which one among the followingis a Buddhist sect

(a) Digambara

(b) Mahayana

(c) Swethambara

(d) Avadhuta

Answer: B

307. Buddhists scripture is known as

(a) Nigama

(b) Pitika

(c) Agama

(d) Karika

Answer: B

308. Which one among the followingis not a Pitika

(a) Visesha

(b) Sutta

(c) Vinaya

(d) Abhidamma

Answer: A

309. Central teaching of Buddhaconsist of Truths

(a) Three

(b) Two

(c) Five

(d) Four

Answer: D

310. Which one among the followingis not a Noble Truth of Buddha

(a) Dukha Marga

(b) Sarvam Dukham

(c) Dukha Nirodha

(d) Dukha Karana

Answer: A